CHRIST
THE FOCAL POINT

The Christ-Centered Life

CHRIST THE FOCAL POINT

The Christ-Centered Life

A Practical Teaching By Dr. Chiemeka Nwokoro

Copyright Information

Christ-The Focal Point
The Christ-Centered Life
By: Dr. Chiemeka Nwokoro

©2018 Published and Copyright by:
Good News Fellowship Ministries

ISBN-13: 978-1-888081-45-9
ISBN-10: 1-888081-45-7

Unless otherwise indicated, all Scripture quotations are from the Authorized King James Version of the Bible.

Printed in the United States of America

Format and Cover Design by Lisa Buck
lisa.joy.buck@gmail.com

Contents

Acknowledgments

Special thanks to my beautiful and loving wife, Ijeoma Nwokoro. Your constant love, prayers and encouragement spurred the birth of this book. My journey in life would be incomplete without you.

- Thanks to my four (4) miracle children, Chinomso, Kelechi, Chiemeka, Jr. ("CJ") and Chidindu. You all inspire me every day and I thank God for blessing me with such wonderful gifts. I love you all more than words can express.

- To my mother, Rose Nwokoro, who has been a source of extra support and inspiration. She taught me diligence and perseverance, which carried me through the writing of this book.

- To my Father Chief Sylverster Nwokoro, my brother Chukwubuike Nwokoro, and my sister Ezinne Uwakwe (nee Nwokoro) who have all supported and encouraged me in various ways through the birth of this book.

- To Rose Shivambo for assisting with review of this book.

- To my Pastor, Dr. Okoji Ndukwe for his encouraging words through-out the process of writing this book.

- To my Professor, Dr. Judy Laidley who empowered me with the spiritual tools and resources needed to birth this book through my Doctoral program at North Carolina College of Theology (NCCT.)

- To everyone who reads this book, may the faith and hope of salvation stretch you beyond the bounds of human limitations.

I thank you all from the depth of my heart and may the blessings of God never depart from your lives.

Dedication

I dedicate this book:

To the Ancient of Days, who
sits upon the throne.

To the Source of our eternal Salvation.

To the Holy Spirit, who dwells
and strengthens us.

And to the angels who upon His
standing commands envelop us.

Introduction

All my life, I have always nurtured a keen curiosity in my heart for the dynamics of Salvation. How Christ's death on the cross of Calvary paved the pathway to eternal Salvation for all who believe in the works of Salvation. "Christ"—The Focal Point is a book inspired by the Holy Spirit who is poised directly to Salvation. This book focuses on the relationship-driven Christianity born out of knowledge and acceptance of Christ's death on the cross, which is the focal point of the New Testament's doors to Salvation. Every chapter of this book stirs up a unique desire to want to know God in a deeper and genuine way. It leads us directly to the image of Christ, the author of our Salvation. I pray and hope that this book will be an inspiration to its readers.

Christ's Ministry

Introduction

In my quest for new discovery with an inept desire to know him more, I approached the topic of Christ's ministry with so much eagerness and expectation. Christ's Ministry is the most intriguing subject matter I have ever written about and the most fascinating of any study I have ever researched in my theological experience. Christ's ministry is the focal point of all history; Christ is the fulfillment of the Old Testament hopes; the source of the New Testament revelation. Jesus Christ is the all in all; hence, the privilege of writing about Christ's ministry is to write about the foundation of the Holy Bible upon which all the promises of salvation are actualized.

Christ's ministry covers the entire account of the life of Jesus from His annunciation to his birth and subsequently highlights the miracles he performed. Jesus was the promised Messiah according to the Old Testament. He was announced as the eternal king who would rise from the lineage of David, who at that time was the king of Israel. Jesus was to come to the world and rescue the people from eternal damnation by his meek submission to the crucifixion on the cross, which signified an eternal bargain for the salvation of all humanity. This chapter will expound on the ministry of Jesus according to the New Testament gospels.

The ministry of Jesus Christ is one that is so exceptional according to its preparation and execution. God prepared for the coming of the Savior of the world by revealing his plans and intentions about the birth of Jesus to his prophets and ministers in the Old Testament. His birth was announced long before He was born, in the book of Isaiah (Isaiah 7:10-14). Isaiah talked about Jesus being named "Immanuel" which is translated to "God with us". The Annunciation was also evidenced by the New Testament in Luke Chapter One:

> *"And behold, you will conceive in your womb*
> *and bring forth a Son, and his name shall be*
> *called Jesus. He will be great and will be called*
> *the Son of the Highest, and the Lord God will*
> *give Him the throne of His father, David. And*
> *He will reign over the house of Jacob forever,*
> *and of His kingdom, there will be no end."*
> *(Luke 1: 31-33).*

This was the preparation for the great ministry of Jesus. The Annunciation was a strong foundation of the ministry as it laid the framework of the ministry that Jesus would have. In the book of Luke, the Angel gave the names that Jesus would bear and that his kingdom would never end. According to Angel Gabriel, Jesus would be a king as his ancestors, David. This brought some friction with the Roman political rulers who governed the people. They saw Jesus' ministry as a "King" to be a threat to their reign and regime.

As evidenced in the New Testament and as commanded in the laws of Moses, Jesus was taken to the temple after his birth as the firstborn. Through the works of the Holy Spirit, the temple priest acknowledged the baby Jesus as the Savior. The old priest (Simeon) had been promised that he would not die without seeing the Messiah. He defined the ministry of Jesus as one that will "experience resistance as many people will speak against him." The priest said to Mary, the mother of Jesus: "the ministry of Jesus would bring the fall and rise of many people" (Luke 2: 34.) It is evident for this reason that the ministry of Jesus was destined to be a daunting mission that would involve a lot of resistance from the rulers and the people. This was talked about while Jesus was a little child and was not even old enough to fathom or comprehend the underlying implication of his assignment. It should be duly noted also that in all, it was obvious that the ministry of Christ was divinely orchestrated and meticulously executed by God. Jesus grew up in the traditional Jewish custom and culture. A tradition that mainly borrowed from the laws of Moses, Jesus used to go to the temple every year with his parents where he listened and learned the scriptures from the teachers of the law. Jesus increased in wisdom and even the teachers of the law were surprised at the knowledge the boy child had as referenced by the scriptures:

"And when he was twelve years old, they went up to Jerusalem after the custom of the feast, and when they had fulfilled the days, as they returned, the child Jesus tarried behind in Jerusalem, and Joseph and his mother knew not, but they supposing him to have been in the company, went a day's journey, and they sought him among their kinsfolk and acquaintance, and when they found him not they turned back again to Jerusalem, seeking him. And it came to pass; that after three days they found him in the temple, sitting in the midst of the doctors, both hearing them and asking them questions, and all that heard him were astonished at his understanding and answers. And when they saw him, they were amazed: and his mother said unto him, Son why hast thou thus dealt

with us? Behold thy father and I have sought thee sorrowing. And he said unto them, how is that ye sought me? Wist ye not that I must be about my father's business?" (Luke 2:42-49.)

Messenger Before Christ

Another incident that showed the divine preparation of the ministry of Christ was the ministry of John the Baptist. John was the Son of Zachariah and the cousin to Jesus and was filled with the Holy Spirit, and sent forth to clear the path before the coming of the Messiah. He was sent to tell of the light of the world which was a symbolic representation of the ministry of Jesus. John preached of a soon coming Messiah, who would baptize people with the Holy Spirit and fire: "John answered, saying unto them all, I indeed baptize you with water, but one mightier than I cometh, the latchet of whose shoes I am not worthy to unloose; he shall baptize you with the Holy Ghost and with fire. Whose fan is in his hand and he will thoroughly purge his floor, and will gather the wheat into his garner, but the chaff he will burn with fire unquenchable." (Luke 3:16-17.) It was through the preaching of John that Jesus came to be baptized. John declared that Jesus was the Messiah he was preparing the way for. He baptized Jesus, and the Spirit of the Lord appeared in the form of a dove, and a voice from the heavens confirmed that Jesus was the son of God:

"Now when all the people were baptized, it came to pass, that Jesus also being baptized, and praying, the heaven was opened and the Holy Ghost descended in a bodily shape like a dove upon him, and a voice came from heaven, which said, thou art my beloved Son, in thee I am well pleased" (Luke 3:21-22.)

John's baptism of Jesus was a crucial event in the order of things, as it created the blueprint and laid the foundation for Christ's ministry.

Baptism

The ministry of Jesus according to the Bible and many theological works, started after he received the baptism from John in the river Jordan. Jesus was thirty years of age, when his ministry took off in his hometown of Galilee. For the works that Jesus did in his ministry were recorded to take part in different historical archives. However, this chapter will flesh out the details surrounding the different phases of Christ's ministry, from the Baptism phase to the early works of Christ, including, but not limited to the Galilean ministry, Judean ministry, ministry of Christ discussing the nature of God and the Heavenly Kingdom and the ministry in Jerusalem, where Jesus concluded His works.

Galilean Ministry of Jesus

Jesus descended from a town called Galilee, which was ruled by a king called Herod. On the day of his baptism, Jesus went from Galilee to the river Jordan, where he met John the Baptist, the son of Zachariah. When John saw him, John was filled with the Holy Spirit and recognized that Jesus was the Messiah prophesied from of old; the one he had been clearing the way for. John proclaimed that Jesus was the light of the world and the lamb of the Lord who takes away the sins of the world. As noted in most theological work, "when John identifies Jesus as the Lamb of God, he was revealing for the very first time, a theology of the role of Jesus Christ, which could very easily be slotted into the Old Testament information about sacrificial lambs. Lambs were at the heart of the sacrificial system of the old covenant (Old Testament). There was the Passover Lamb offered once per year, as a sin offering in the fullest sense (Exodus 12 : 12 - 13). There were also the lambs of burnt offering - the morning and evening sacrifices every day and twice on the Sabbaths (Leviticus 1 : 4). Then there was the lamb of the 'trespass offering' which was offered as required, when some particular defilement excluded a person from attending worship. So, in all of these cases, lambs were sacrificed to provide 'legal purification' for ceremonial defilement. They visibly demonstrated the need for atonement in order to remove the pollution and penalty of sin, and to effect reconciliation between God and sinners." Jesus was baptized by John, and after the baptism, the Spirit of the Lord descended upon him and in the form of a dove and the heaven opened and said that Jesus was the Son of God that He is pleased with. This was a fulfillment of the words that were spoken by the Angel Gabriel to the Mother of Jesus, Mary (Matthew 3: 16-17). It is recorded that after Jesus was baptized by John, he was taken into the wilderness by the spirit, where he did not eat for forty days and forty nights. Jesus was tempted by the devil in preparation and anticipation of starting the hard task of his ministry which as recorded, would face strong opposition (Köstenberger, Andreas, Kellum, and Quarles, 140). Jesus was tempted three times and overcame the temptations, and after that, he came back to Galilee and started his early ministry: "then was Jesus led up of the spirit into the wilderness to be tempted of the devil, and when he had fasted forty days and forty nights, he was afterwards hungered and when the tempter came to him, he said, if thou be the son of God, command that these stones be made bread, but he answered and said man shall not live by bread alone, but by every word that proceedeth out of the mouth of God..."(Mathew 4:1-11). Research shows that the three different temptations as evidenced in Jesus' wilderness experience represented: (1)the lust of the flesh, wherein the devil asked him to turn the rocks into bread to fulfill his earthly cravings; (2) lust of the eyes, in which case the devil promised to give him "all the kingdoms of the world" and finally (3) Pride of life, where the devil asked him to cast himself down before the appointed time of God.

Rejection of Christ in his Hometown

Christ's rejection by his own hometown kinsmen was a fulfilment of scriptures. Jesus' popularity spread all over the lands, and when he met John the Baptist again, John proclaimed him as the lamb of the Lord and two of his disciples followed Jesus. Jesus called some other disciples who followed him. In His early works, Jesus preached the good news of the kingdom of God in the synagogues where everyone praised him for his wisdom. Jesus preached all over the locality, and he once went to the town he grew up in, Nazareth, and he read the scriptures. He read from the scroll of Isaiah where it is written that the Spirit of the Lord is upon him and has chosen him to proclaim the good news to the poor and set the captives free. He affirmed to the people that He is the promised Messiah who would deliver them from captivity and usher a kingdom that will never end (Luke 4:18-21). At this time, the Jews were under the Roman rule which had colonized them. According to their custom and expectation, they anticipated a Messiah who would from past precedent present as a political leader and raise a strong army to defeat their oppressors. The people were angry with Jesus at Nazareth, as they knew him as the son of Joseph the carpenter. The people could not figure out how the carpenter's son would usher a kingdom that is everlasting and a kingdom that could conquer the whole world. They also resisted the true identity of Jesus as the Son of God, and accused him of blasphemy. The officials took Jesus to a tall cliff and were planning to kill him, but Jesus through divine intervention walked through their midst and went away as indicated in the scriptures:

> *"and all they in the Synagogue, when they heard these things, were filled with wrath, and rose up, and thrust him out of the city, and led him unto the brow of the hill whereon their city was built, that they might cast him down headlong. But he passing through the midst went his way" (Luke 4:28-30).*

This was a representation of the task that was ahead of Him to convince the people of his true nature. The people rejected him as a form of the prophesied resistance by the old priest Simeon.

Healing the Sick and Other Miracles

The early ministry of Jesus was characterized by the works of miracles he performed by healing the sick and delivering salvation to the lost. It was in this early ministry that Jesus healed Simon's mother in law and so many other sick people. Jesus also cast out demons, and the demons upon leaving their oppressed, proclaimed Jesus as the Son of God. Many people believed in the good news, and the way Jesus taught showed that he had the understanding of the religious matters. Some people compared the teaching of the teachers of the law to that of Jesus, and they concluded that Jesus taught well and he taught with authority. According to the book of Matthew,

> *"and so it was, when Jesus had ended these sayings, that the people were astonished at His teaching, for He taught them as one having authority, and not as the scribes." (Matthew 7: 28-29).*

Jesus in this early ministry turned water into wine at Cana in Galilee and also performed many miracles in Capernaum. "And there were set there six water pots of stone, after the manner of the purifying of the Jews, containing two or three firkins apiece, Jesus saith unto them, fill the water pots with water, and they filled it up to the brim, and he saith unto them draw out near, and bear unto the governor of the feast, and they bare it. When the ruler of the feast had tasted the water that was made wine, and knew not whence it was (but the servants which drew the water knew) the governor of the feast called the bridegroom and saith unto him,

"everyman at the beginning doth set forth good
wine, and when men are well drunk, then that
which is worse: but thou hast kept the good
wine until now" (John 2:6-10.)

His popularity spread like wild fire and Jesus also showed wonders to his disciples. He called many disciples from different professions and statuses. He once told the disciples including Simon Peter to cast their nets into a sea where they had caught nothing overnight and to their surprise, they caught a significant number of fish such that their nets were unable to hold and forcing them to ask for help. This miracle signified that the supernatural power Christ had, exceeded natural boundaries over every living thing and that he reigned in all the living and non-living by defying the laws of nature and science. Based on the miracles ascertained by his divine nature, Jesus then told the fishermen who later became his disciple that if they followed Him, they would become fishers of men. Jesus also talked about the kingdom of God through the Sermon on the Mount in the book of Matthew and sermon on the plain in the book of Luke.

After Jesus had preached of the blessings and the woes that each person would receive in the everlasting kingdom, the ministry gets into another phase of the Galilean ministry, which is known as the "Great Galilean Ministry." This is marked by actions and events that occurred before the death of John the Baptist. This segment of the ministry is marked by Jesus' completion of the spreading of the good news to the people and being called by a Roman officer who beckoned to Jesus, petitioning him to heal his servant. The officer had a sick servant whom he loved dearly. He sent for Jesus through the Jewish elders that Jesus would heal his servant. The servant was a good man and had built a synagogue for the Jews, and Jesus agreed to go with them. While on the way, the officer sent words to Jesus stating "only say a word and my servant would be healed," as the officer did not feel worthy to receive or even meet Jesus. Jesus was astonished by the amount of faith the officer exhibited, and proceeded to teach his disciples about faith being an important virtue, Jesus healed the servant through sending the word,

> *"...wherefore neither thought I myself to come unto thee; but say in a word and my servant shall be healed. For I also as a man set under authority, having under me soldiers, and I say unto one, Go and he goeth, and to another, come and he cometh; and to my servant, do this and he doeth it, when Jesus heard these things, he marveled at him, and turned him about, and said unto the people that followed him, I say unto you, I have not found so great faith, no, not in Israel. And they that were sent, returning to the house, found the servant whole that had been sick" (Luke 7:1-10).*

Jesus portrayed a very powerful person as it was a miracle that a person could recover by just saying the words. At this point, it is evident that Jesus had done so many wonders that proved he was divinely sent and not just a carpenter's son. This is quite clear as the Roman officer was a Gentile, yet he had more faith than the Jews.

Jesus and His Disciples

Jesus' ministry continued to grow in leaps and bounds. On a certain day, after ministering to the people, Jesus got on a boat with his disciples. When sailing through the Sea of Galilee, Jesus fell asleep. While asleep on the boat, there was a great storm, and the disciples were terrified that the boat would capsize and everyone aboard would drown. They proceeded to wake Jesus and in their despair told him to save them. Jesus felt sorry for them, and he asked them why they had so little faith. Jesus ordered the winds and the storms to cease, and there was complete calmness. The people and the disciples were so amazed by the divinity of Jesus that nature obeyed his command. Jesus taught them to have faith and fear not:

"And when he was entered into a ship, his dis-
ciples followed him. And behold, there arose a
great tempest in the sea, insomuch that the ship
was covered with the waves: but he was asleep.
And his disciples came to him, and awoke him
saying, Lord, save us: we perish. And he saith
unto them, why are ye fearful, O ye of little
faith? Then he arose and rebuked the winds
and the sea, and there was calm. But the men
marveled, saying, what manner of man is this,
that even the winds and the sea obey him"
(Mathew 8:23-27.)

Faith was a strong pillar in the ministry of Christ.

The Galilean ministry continues with Jesus calling more disciples to go with him and to proclaim the good news of the Kingdom of God, Matthew was called to the ministry of Christ in this section, Jesus found Matthew in his office as a tax collector, and Jesus told him to follow him. Matthew followed Jesus, and they came to dine in the house of Matthew. Many tax collectors came to the house and ate with Jesus. The Pharisees were not happy with Jesus for eating with the tax collectors, as they were viewed as sinners. Upon hearing them, Jesus spoke in parables, giving an analogy of only the sick needing a doctor:

*"And when the Pharisees saw it, they said to
His disciples, "Why does your Teacher eat with
tax collectors and sinners?" When Jesus heard
that, He said to them, "and it came to pass, as
Jesus sat at meat in the house, behold, many
publicans and sinners came and sat down with
him and his disciples. And when the Pharisees
saw it, they said unto his disciples, why eateth
your master with publicans and sinners? But
when Jesus heard that, he said unto them, they
that are whole need not a physician, but they
that are sick. But go ye and learn what that
meaneth, I will have mercy, and not sacrifice;
for I am not come to call righteous, but sinners
to repentance."(Matthew 9:10-13).*

Jesus' comment in the above-mentioned parable showed
that He came to save the whole world and not to save a particular sect of people. He came to find the lost in his ministry and
not for the righteous, and would readily leave the ninety-nine
righteous to get the one lost. In this part of Christ's ministry,
Jesus taught the people about the kingdom using many parables such as the parable of the mustard seed, the sower, and
the hidden treasure among others. Jesus also commissioned
the apostles to go to different places where they preached the
gospel and worked miracles in the name of Jesus. He instructed them not to carry anything as they would be given food
and shelter wherever they went. Jesus expressed that the kingdom of heaven is not materialistic by sending his followers to
spread the gospel without carrying any supplies (Matthew, and
Clark, 1814). In the conclusion of the Great Galilean Ministry,
Jesus returned to his hometown of Nazareth where people
knew him and where he faced much opposition.

The Galilean Ministry continues to the final phase where Jesus does many works, and this takes place after the demise of John the Baptist. It was in this phase that Jesus fed the five thousand people using five loaves of bread and two fish (Mathew 14:13-21). Jesus also performed extraordinary miracles in this phase such as walking on water. While in the water, his disciples saw him, and were petrified. In fact, they thought that he was a ghost. Peter, one of his disciples, told him to order him to walk on water if he was Jesus and not a ghost. Jesus asked him to come while walking on water. Peter set his feet on the water and walked towards Jesus and did not sink. He was surprised, and due to what Jesus regarded as little faith, Peter started to sink, but Jesus caught him by hand and helped him (Mark 6:45-52, Matthew 14:22-23 and John 6:16-21). This was a good portrayal of Jesus conquering the laws of nature, as he was divine and not bound by nature as the son of God. He also taught the disciples the works of faith and the importance of having steadfast faith in the works of God. Jesus cleansed the ten lepers and healed the daughter of the Canaanite woman who was possessed by a demon. Jesus emphasized of the power of having faith. Jesus also taught of the things that make a person unclean. He described that the things that go into a person cannot make him or her unclean. He stated that the things that make people unclean are the things that get out from the person. The ministry at Galilee is concluded by the question to his disciples of who people said he was. Different answers were given by the disciples, and finally, Jesus asked them who they said he was. Peter answered him that he was the Messiah.

"When Jesus came into the coasts of Caesarea Phillipi, he asked his disciples, saying, whom do men say that I the Son of man am? And they said some say that thou art John the Baptist: some say Elias, and others Jeremias, or one of the prophets. He saith unto them but whom say ye that I am? And Simon Peter answered and

said, Thou art Christ, the Son of the living God"
(Mathew 16:13-16.)

The Judean Ministry

Jesus Talks of His Death

The beginning of Christ's ministry in Judea was characterized by the prediction of his death. He had fore warned his disciples of the torment that he, as the Christ would undergo as
part of his ministry to fulfill his destiny. He told the disciples
of the rejection he was to face and the opposition in spreading
the word of God. He was to be opposed by the teachers of the
law and the high priests as part of fulfilling the works of his
ministry.

> *"From that time Jesus began to show to His dis-*
> *ciples that He must go to Jerusalem, and suffer*
> *many things from the elders and chief priests*
> *and scribes, and be killed, and be raised the*
> *third day" (Mark 8:31-33 and Matthew 16:21-*
> *28.)*

Transfiguration

About a week after Jesus spoke to the disciples about his
death, he went with some of his disciples up on a mountain for
prayers. He took Peter, James, and John and as he was praying, he changed in facial appearance, and his clothes turned
dazzling white. At that moment, two men appeared, and they
started talking to Jesus. One of the men was Elijah, and the
other one was Moses. This was symbolic in the sense that Jesus' ministry was a representative of both the prophets and the
deuterocanonical laws.

"And after six days Jesus taketh Peter, James and John his brother, and bringeth them up unto an high mountain apart, and was transfigured before them: his face did shine as the sun, and his raiment was white as the light. And behold, there appeared unto them Moses and Elias talking with him" (Mathew 17:1-3.)

It showed that Jesus did not come to destroy the laws of Moses or the works of the early prophets but instead came to reinforce and fulfill them. The two men talked with Jesus of the way Christ's mission would be fulfilled by Jesus dying on the cross to cleanse the whole world. It was a clear indication that the ministry of Jesus was not a fiction. It was an indication that there is life after death as the two men had died long ago, but were alive, having died while in faithful service to God. The disciples witnessed the men leaving and Peter told Jesus that they would build three tents, one for him and the two for the two prophets. In that moment, when Peter was still speaking during the transfiguration, the heavens opened in the form of cloud and once more, the voice re-affirmed that Jesus was God's son whom he had chosen (Matthew 17:1-6.) The transfiguration as termed, gave Jesus the encouragement that God was with him and that the ministry would be fulfilled by Jesus dying on the cross. "The word "transfigured" is a very interesting word. The Greek word is "metamorpho" and it means to transform, literally or figuratively to metamorphose, or to change. The word is a verb that means to change into another form. It also means to change the outside to match the inside. The prefix "meta" means to change and the "morphe" means form. In the case of the transfiguration of Jesus Christ it means to match the outside with the reality of the inside. To change the outward so that it matches the inward reality. Jesus' divine nature was "veiled" in human form and the transfiguration was a glimpse of that glory. Therefore, the transfiguration of Jesus Christ displayed the Shekinah glory of God incarnate in the Son. The voice of God attesting to the truth of Jesus' Sonship was the second time God's voice was heard. The first time was at Jesus' baptism into His public ministry by John the Baptist" The event also gave the disciples the motivation to follow in the shoes of Jesus in spreading the word of God as they heard that Jesus was the son of God and witnessed what happened. Jesus ordered the disciples not to speak of their vision to anyone which indicates that Christ's ministry would continue even after his persecution. The transfiguration was also a clear indication that the real identity of Jesus was no longer a secret to his disciples and also in this ministry, Jesus death and persecutions is emphasized a lot as part of God's plan.

Preparation for Jesus' Death

In this section of the ministry of Jesus, there was the question of appointment of who would take charge of the other disciples in facilitating the spread of the good news. It should be duly noted that the term "good news," means "to bring or announce good news." It is derived from the noun "angelos," or "messenger." In classical Greek, an euangelos was one who brought a message of victory or other political or personal news that caused joy, "to speak as a messenger of gladness, to proclaim good news."Following the certain truth about Jesus fulfilling his destiny by his death on the cross, there was a need to appoint an heir to take charge over the work of Christ. Jesus appointed Peter to succeed the leadership over the other disciples. The appointment came after Peter declared that Jesus was the promised Messiah. The appointment of Peter showed that Jesus was ready and knew the task he had to fulfill. It also shows that He was a great official in the kingdom of heaven. This was exhibited through the authority by which he discussed this new role with Peter. It is also reflected in the words or rather the promise he gave Peter, decreeing that Peter was endeared with the power to bind, curse and to bless and do many other things as Jesus did. The things the disciples would bind on earth would be bound in heaven. This shows the continuity of Jesus' ministry even after his death and resurrection. Jesus also talks of Peter being a rock upon which he would build his church. The symbol of a rock is a strong foundation that would become the stronghold of the ministry. This shows that Jesus wanted the disciples to spread the word after him.

> *"Jesus answered and said to him, "Blessed are you, Simon Bar-Jonah, for flesh and blood have not revealed this to you, but My Father who is in heaven. And I also say to you that you are Peter, and on this rock, I will build my church, and the gates of Hades shall not prevail against it. And I will give you the keys of the kingdom of heaven, and whatever you bind on earth will be bound in heaven, and whatever you loose on earth will be loosed in heaven." Then He commanded His disciples that they should tell no one that He was Jesus the Christ." (Matthew 16:17-20.)*

Jesus talked about his journey to Jerusalem, and he talked again about his death. He performed many miracles that included healing the sick and casting out demons.

Ministry of Christ About the Nature of God and the Heavenly Kingdom

In this part of Christ's ministry, Jesus talked about the church community that would be administered by the disciples and other apostles of Christ. Jesus talked about the nature of God and the Heavenly Kingdom, this part of Jesus' ministry included the parables that showed his real mission, which included the parable of the lost sheep and the parable of the unforgiving servant. In the parable of the lost sheep, (Luke15: 4-7), Jesus gave an example of a man who had a hundred sheep. Jesus explained that if one of the hundred sheep got lost, the man would leave the ninety-nine grazing and go in search for the lost one. He would be much happier by finding the one that was lost, rather than the ninety-nine that did not get lost.

"I say unto you, that likewise joy shall be in heaven over one sinner that repenteth, more than over ninety and nine just persons, which need no repentance." (Luke 15:7.)

The parable described how excited God gets when a lost soul is won back to him than the ones that are already His. The Kingdom of Heaven was that of mercy and forgiveness as portrayed by Jesus in the parable of the unforgiving servant who desired to be forgiven but could not forgive others. Jesus explained the parable that there was once a wealthy king who upon reviewing his business books discovered that there was a servant who owed him a lot of money and the king ordered that the servant be brought before him. The servant had no money to pay the debt and the king ordered that the servant be sold together with his belongings and all his family to settle the debt. The servant pleaded earnestly with the king and he was forgiven the debt. After a while the servant who had been forgiven found a fellow servant who owed him a small amount of money and even after beseeching for more time, refused to forgive the minor debt owed by the fellow servant. But instead mistreated his colleague and finally had him locked up in jail. The news reached the king who became furious and ordered the forgiven servant to be jailed. "Should you not also have had compassion on your fellow servant, just as I had pity on you?' And his master was angry and delivered him to the torturers until he should pay all that was due to him. So My heavenly Father also will do to you if each of you, from his heart, does not forgive his brother his trespasses." (Matthew 18:33-35.)

The take away from the parable was that God would not forgive people if they do not forgive others. This shows that the ministry of Jesus was built on penance and forgiveness (Matthew 18: 21-35.)

The final major event in this part of Jesus' ministry was the act of raising Lazarus of Bethany from the dead. Lazarus had been dead for a number of days and buried before Jesus showed up.

"Jesus therefore again groaning in himself cometh to the grave. It was a cave, and a stone laid upon it. Jesus said take ye away the stone. Martha, the sister of him that was dead, saith unto him, Lord, by this time he stinketh: for he hath been dead four days. Jesus saith unto her, said I not unto thee that, if thou wouldest believe thou shouldest see the glory of God? Then they took away the stone from the place where the dead was laid. And Jesus lifted up his eyes, and said, Father, I thank thee that thou hast heard me. And I knew that thou hearest me always: but because of the people which stand by I said it, that they may believe that thou hast sent me. And when he thus had spoken, he cried with a loud voice, Lazarus, come forth. And he that was dead came forth, bound hand and foot with grave clothes, and his face was bound about with a napkin. Jesus said unto them loose him and let him go" (John 11:38-44.)

In obedience to his command, Lazarus who had been dead for a number of days came back to life and the multitudes were filled with amazement. This was done to show that Jesus had power over death and the grave.

Christ's Ministry in Jerusalem

Triumphant Entry to Jerusalem

Christ's ministry in Jerusalem was marked by the triumphant entry into Jerusalem at the start of the ministry and the end characterized by the crucifixion of Jesus. In the triumphant entry, Jesus sent his disciples to go and bring a donkey and her colt tied in a village ahead. Jesus rode on the colt and while he was entering Jerusalem, people spread out their cloaks on the road for the colt to step on. This was symbolic because many people had believed in the divine nature of Jesus and they had accepted him as the redeemer of the world through the mighty works he had performed. However, Jesus riding on the colt was a fulfillment of the ancient prophecy of the Messiah being king of the world. He expressed his humility in the service of the ministry (Matthew 21: 1-11.)

Cleansing of the Church

After Jesus had entered Jerusalem in glory, he went to the temple, where he found people doing business in the temple, and he was angry. He drove them out and rebuked them, cautioning that the temple is a place of prayer and not a "hide out" for thieves. He taught in the temple and the more he taught, the more the teachers of the law and other leaders wanted to kill him. They even came together to challenge Him asking under whose authority Jesus did the miracles. Jesus perceived their odious thoughts and refused to tell them under whose authority he performed miracles (Luke 19: 45-48, 20: 1-8.) The leaders and the chief priests were afraid of Jesus' popularity and his ability to attract the crowd, which was a threat to their teachings. Jesus reprimanded the hypocrisy of the Pharisees and other Jewish leaders. It was at this phase of Christ's ministry that he was betrayed by a notable disciple. Jesus was tested by the leaders through tough questions that would form the basis for his arrest and ultimate crucifixion on the cross. The Pharisees and teachers of the law sought so desperately to arrest Jesus. They used devious antics and tricks, but to no avail. Jesus overcame all their tricks, and they were troubled:

> *"and the chief priests and the scribes the same hour sought to lay hands on him: and they feared the people: for they perceived that he had spoken these parables against them. And they watched him, and sent forth spies, which should feign themselves just men, and they might take hold of his words, that so they might deliver him unto the power and authority of the governor. And they asked him, saying Master, we know that thou sayest and teachest rightly, neither acceptest thou the person of any, but teachest the way God truly is: is it lawful for us to give tribute unto Caesar, or not, but he perceived there craftiness and said unto them, why tempt ye me?......" (Luke 20:19-26.)*

Jesus preached, and in this part of his ministry, he did not perform many miracles. He taught of the things to come and mostly about his persecution. The event that is prevalent in this ministry of Jerusalem is where Jesus instituted the Eucharist by having the last supper with the disciples. He shared bread and wine which symbolized the body and blood of Christ. He went to pray later on after the meal, and he was arrested and crucified after betrayal by Judas. As prophesied, Jesus was persecuted harshly and shamefully and even denied for the sake of fulfilling his mission of saving mankind from sin. The ministry of Christ ends in Jerusalem where he died in the hands of the Jewish leaders and the priests. After his death, Jesus rose on the third day and ascended into heaven. His disciples were instructed to continue with the work of spreading the gospel after Christ (Luke 22-24.)

Conclusion

The ministry of Christ was a tough task as it was a total opposite of what they expected. They expected a mighty ruler in appearance, who would conquer nations through military power, but instead, Jesus was a humble religious king. The people opposed him as it was prophesied, because the people had a different belief system. Jesus never ostracized anyone, but associated with everybody including sinners as a way to close the bridge and win more souls to the Kingdom of heaven. In doing so, Jesus showed that forgiveness of sins was part of his ministry. Jesus in his ministry preached of peace of mind and about the light of the body. In his teachings, he emphasized the power of faith, humility, and sacrifice so that one can have eternal life. He was also an advocate for the kingdom of heaven as one that was not materialistic. Material possession was portrayed as a stumbling block to entering the heavenly kingdom. Christ preached against hypocrisy and all other social injustices in the world and instituted a kingdom of justice and love for others. His ministry was a success with the disciples taking over after him in spreading the good news without fear of persecution. They advocated for truth and justice for all and they became the light of the gospel as Christ prepared them.

Jesus Christ is not only the standard of righteousness; He is also the source of it. He is both the pattern and provision for the Christian walk. It was the death of Christ which saved us from sin in the past and it is the life of Christ which delivers us from sin in the present and future and note the ministry of Christ records the authentication of Jesus Christ as Messiah, his presentation of Himself and His rejection by His own people, all of these things fulfilled the old testament prophecies about the Messiah.

Jesus Christ is the most important person in all recorded history. Jesus Christ is God's provision for man's sin, Jesus died in the sinner's place.

"He who was sinless took man's sin upon Himself and suffered the penalty of God's wrath for all who believe," (2 Cor 5:21).

He provides every believer with His righteousness so that we may spend eternity with God (Rom. 3:21-26) but in addition to Christ's ministry He is the example, He is the standard of righteousness for all who believe. Our trials and tests He knows, for He was tempted in all regards, yet came out with flying colors without any sin or blemish(Hebrews 4:15.) The life of Jesus is the pattern for a solid and fulfilled Christian conduct (1 Peter 2:21.)

When you stand before Him at the judgment throne of God, you will not be asked what church you attended and how often were you in church every Sunday, or how much money you earned or gave to people, or whether you were baptized or not? God will ask only one thing, what did you do about my Son Jesus Christ? Have you trusted In Him as your Lord and personal savior? Do you believe what He did for your sins? Are you resting in His righteousness for Gods approval? To have Him, is to have eternal life.

"He that hath the son hath life, and he that hath not the son of God hath not life."

Christ ministry sets the pedestal and shows the way to Him in order for man to have everlasting life and a joyful life on this earth.

In order for this conclusion on Christ's ministry to be complete, I have to invite you to accept Jesus Christ as your savior. You must accept Jesus into your life. Just say this short prayer and he will come into your life and dwell in you. You also need to understand that we all are sinners; "for all have sinned."

We just need to turn to the Lord Jesus Christ for forgiveness of sins by repenting of our sins. Confess Jesus as your savior

Romans 10:13: "For whosoever shall call upon the name of the Lord shall be saved".

Lord Jesus, I ask you to forgive my sins and save me from eternal separation from God. By faith, I accept your ministry and death on the cross as sufficient payment for my sins. Thank You for providing the way for me to know You and to have a relationship with my heavenly Father. Through faith in You, I have eternal life. Thank You also for hearing my prayers and loving me unconditionally. Please give me the strength, wisdom, and determination to walk in the center of Your will, In Jesus' name, amen.

The Kingdom of Heaven

Introduction

This chapter really makes me happy; because the Kingdom of heaven is the earnest desire of every believer in Christ, so I feel very privileged and delighted to write a chapter on it. Before I proceed, I would like to first note that the Kingdom of heaven will be used interchangeable with the Kingdom of God, and this Kingdom will be used with a capitalized letter "K." Definition of the word kingdom: the word kingdom is translated from the Greek word basileia - it refers to the realm, dimension, principality or empire, it presupposes a monarch a king or queen, it may refer to a country ruled by a monarch, and Kingdom of Heaven is simply the rule of God. The complete and total rule of God will come when, in the future, the Kingdom of the world has become the Kingdom of Our Lord and Christ. But note that this total submission is to be experienced now by those who receive Jesus Christ as Savior and Lord. So in other words, the only way to make it to the Kingdom of Heaven is by accepting Jesus as your personal Savior and by so doing, we will have everlasting life and we will dwell in the Kingdom of heaven.

"For God so loved the world that He gave his only begotten Son, that whosoever believeth in him should not perish, but have everlasting life." John 3:16

So from the above introduction I have ascertained that the only way to the Kingdom of heaven is through Jesus Christ the Son of God, and also in John 3:3, Jesus Himself stated it clearly: "Jesus answered and said unto him, verily, verily, I say unto thee, Except a man be born again, he cannot see the kingdom of God. And also looking at the central message that made up the basis for Jesus entire ministry and teachings, He pinpointed this central message in the heart of His sermon on the mount, and he also made it clear, what should be the highest priority of His followers. According to Matthew 6:33

"But seek first the kingdom of God and His righteousness, and all these things shall be added to you."

And Jesus Christ's words were clear that God is to be the first focus and emphasis in the lives of His followers. In short, this is the core gospel of his message, and before any of this things could be achieved, we should have a personal relationship with God by being born-again and continually striving to seek his Kingdom. By God's grace, Heaven will be our sure destination (Born Again +always seeking His Kingdom = Making it into the Kingdom of God.) This goes further to explain in greater detail how one can get to the Kingdom of God. It begins with a personal conversion as depicted in John 3:3, Col 1:13, without conversion, it is impossible to get our inheritance and reward in the Kingdom of heaven. After the conversion we must recognize that Jesus Christ is the only way to salvation and to the Kingdom of heaven.

The kingdom of Heaven requires the following:

The Kingdom of heaven requires commitment, obedience and preparation. A typical example of the kingdom of heaven is seen in the parable of the ten virgins and the parable of the talents in Matthew 25. As noted in this chapter, the Kingdom is kept for those who hear and prepare and commit to the path of salvation. The Kingdom is God's gift to us and as believers; we must not become passive and lazy in being prayerful and watchful. The greatness of the gift calls for a life of the most strenuous vigilance, effort, and radical obedience. It is the ultimate gift given to us, and so, we must give the ultimate allegiance to God's Kingdom.

The Kingdom of heaven is also very expensive we can see how expensive it is in the following bible passage Mathew 13:44-46:

"Again the Kingdom of heaven is like unto a treasure hid in the field, which when a man hath found, he hideth, and for joy thereof goeth and selleth all that he hath and buyeth that field, Again the Kingdom of heaven is like unto a merchant man seeking goodly pearls, who when he had found one pearl of great price, went and sold all that he had, and bought it."

As indicated in the above-mentioned bible verse, we can also see that we have to give up all that we have including our own dear life for the Kingdom of heaven, because this Kingdom is the highest of all Kingdoms, and when we are there, there will be no more worries, tribulation, frustration, confusion or mistakes, and we must pay dearly for this Kingdom.

Conclusion

God's Kingdom is near to each believer, and before anyone can experience or enter into this Kingdom, it definitely starts with a conversion, which implies a transformation and being born again. The concept of conversion is broadly construed to apply to as many that sincerely abandon their ungodly beliefs and principles; embracing the transformative power of God through salvation. It should be noted that only those who are born again through the power of salvation can enter the Kingdom of God. Jesus Christ is the sole ruler in this Kingdom, and in Matthew 18 : 3-4:

> *"And said verily I say unto you except ye be converted and become as little children, ye shall not enter into the Kingdom of heaven, whosoever therefore shall humble himself as this little child the same is greatest in the Kingdom of heaven."*

According to the above-mentioned bible passage, conversion is a very important process to being one with God. It requires a meek and clean heart (no grudges, no envy, no slandering, no stealing, no killing, no back biting etc) it requires a heart like a new born child. In order to make it to heaven, we should also anticipate tribulations and persecutions here on earth. Like Jesus, we must go through hardship, tribulation and persecution as indicated in Acts14:22.

> *"Confirming the souls of the disciples, and exhorting them to continue in the faith, and that we must go through much tribulation to enter into the Kingdom of God."*

This price we must pay through our journey of salvation with a reward of spending eternal life with our Lord and savior Jesus Christ.

Heaven

- What Can We Know About it Now?

Introduction

This chapter is very exhilarating, because it is my innate and sole desire to make it to heaven. Luke 23:43 gives a descriptive overview of the kingdom of God:

> "And Jesus said unto him verily verily I say unto thee, today shalt thou be with me in paradise (heaven)."

The book of Rev 21:1 also gives a brief view into the heavenly kingdom:

> "I saw a new heaven and a new earth: for the first heaven and the first earth were passed away and there was no more sea."

Looking at these two bible passages it is obvious that heaven is real. As both passages were written in different times and eras, yet are confirmatory of the presence of heaven. The first bible verse projects a welcoming scenario, where Christ welcomed someone into heaven. The second passage confirms the unfading nature of heaven. Heaven symbolizes our final and permanent home (Rev 21 and 22) and the opposite is hell—the final and permanent place for the lost (Matt 25:41)

How are we going to get into this heaven? During the second coming of Jesus, Christ will come to execute judgment and be glorified in his people, during which there will be a final judgment throne before which all will stand to give an account of the life once lived, and rewards will be given to the saved as described in Revelations 20:12:

> *"and I saw the dead, small and great stand before God, and the books were opened: and another book was opened, which is the book of life, and the dead were judged out of those things which were written in the books, according to their works."*

In that moment, a final directive will be given and each person will either be welcome into heaven or cast into hell and eternal damnation and there will be no middle ground or in between.

Why Judgment?

1. Judgment is a reminder that this world is not our home, our citizenship is in heaven according to Phil 3:20 "For our conversation is in heaven, from whence also we look for the savior, the Lord Jesus Christ."

2. Judgment evokes a sense of purpose. It makes us understand that the main purpose of the gospel is to keep us fit for heaven. John 3:16 says "for God so loved the world that he gave his only begotten son, that whosoever believeth in him should not perish,

but have everlasting life." From this passage we must give our life to Christ and constantly believe in him and have faith in him, for us to have this everlasting life, which we will be spending in heaven.

3. To give us the zeal and hunger for things eternal, looking deeply or else we will become so attached to this life 1 John 2:15-17 "Love not the world, neither the things that are in the world. If any man love the world, the love of the father is not with him, for all that is in the world, the lust of the flesh, and the lust of the eyes, and the pride of life, is not of the father, but of the world. The world passeth away and the lust thereof: but he that doeth the will of God abideth for ever". So when we simply do the will of God, the things He wants us to do, heaven will definitely be our portion.

4. For many Christians that feel cheated in this life, because of lack of good health, money and all other good things which this life brings, we will be rewarded in our future home which is heaven, were there will be no hunger, lack etc Romans 8:18 "For I reckon that the sufferings of this present time are not worthy to be compared with the glory which shall be revealed in us"

5. It also focuses on the many things on which the bible is very clear, so that we may know that the hope set before us is based upon the objective and the truth of God's word, which are all biblical facts.

6. And most importantly we should know that the accuser of brethren Satan is always there to stall us and to make us, in any way not to make heaven, in john 10:10 it boldly says that "The thief (Satan) cometh to steal, and to kill and to destroy: I am come that they might have life and they might have it more abundantly.

What Will the Experience of Heaven be Like?

Now we have known the basis of this chapter, we will now delve into the more interesting part, which is what will heaven be like?

1. The first and foremost thing to note is that heaven is a place as stated in Rev. 21:2 "And I John saw the holy city, new Jerusalem, coming down from God out of heaven, prepared as a bride adorned for her husband." Heaven is the dwelling place of God, and Jesus promised to prepare a place for true Christians in heaven (John 14:2). Heaven is also the destination of Old testament saints who died trusting Gods promise of the redeemer. And we already know that whoever believes in Christ shall not perish but have eternal life (John 3:16) and this eternal life will be spent in this particular and awesome place called "heaven."

2. Heaven is a place of rest from this world struggles, there will be no more tears, no more pain and no more sorrows (Rev 21:4), there will be no more separation, because death will be forever conquered (Rev. 20:6).

3. Heaven symbolizes a place of union between God and man. A place where God will dwell with us and we with God; a place of direct daily communion with God. Heaven is a place of daily devotion in the presence of God and every believer must aspire to make it to there.

4. Heaven is a celestial place, where the early bodies of believers will be perpetually transformed; we will have new bodies and new minds, our body will be like that of Jesus, our minds will be without evil, no envy or rival spirit will dwell in Heaven (1 Con 15:52)

5. Heaven as stated in number one is a place we will
    meet the saints face to face. I can't wait to meet the
    people I have read about in the bible like David,
    Solomon, Job etc, and we can only meet this entire
    people in heaven.

6. Heaven is a place that transcends our imaginations,
    and the beauty is incomparable, the building walls
    are of Jasper, and the city is pure gold, and the walls
    of the city are garnished with all manner of precious
    stones, and the gates are of pearls, (Rev: 10-26) the
    beauty is beyond any earthly beauty.

7. In heaven we will not be subject to the laws of phys-
    ics, in John 20: 19-26, we find Jesus walking through
    walls and locked doors, and in heaven we will be able
    to do all that, there will be no physical barriers.

8. Heaven will be a place of perfect worship, a place
    where believers never get tired of worshipping and
    praising God.

The Way to Heaven

The cross is the only way to heaven. A believer aspiring to
make it to heaven must first believe in the work of Salvation—
the crucifixion of our Lord Jesus Christ on the cross of Calvary.
Having discussed the chapter on Heaven, we have come to understand that heaven is God's home, God is perfect, nothing
imperfect can ever enter heaven, Romans 3:23 says,

> *"For all have sinned, and come short of the glo-
> ry of God."*

But the Almighty God gave us a bridge to cover that gap
between us and God, which is JESUS. John 3:16 says,

"For God so loved the world, that he gave his only begotten Son, that whosoever believeth in him should not perish but have everlasting life"

Jesus died on the cross for our sins, He took our punishment for sinning, and offers forgiveness to us, all we need to do is acknowledge that we are sinners and ask for forgiveness and accept him as our Lord and personal Savior and we will definitely make Heaven.

A Prayer of Repentance—Say this Prayer

Lord I realized that I am a sinner, thank you for sending your Son, Jesus to die on the cross of Calvary for my sins, I accept Jesus right now as my Lord and Savior, please show me your will and help me become exactly the person you want me to become, in JESUS name I pray. Amen.

Conclusion

Heaven is the final destination for all who believe in the work of salvation and the crucifixion of Jesus. Heaven is a believer's reward for obedience here on earth A place created by God for his children.

"For by him all things were created, in heaven and on earth, visible and invisible."

And it is an eternal home of every believer, born again Christians, no matter the age or race or any other individual attributes, and there will be no sin, pain or sorrow in heaven, Satan, the accuser of brethren, has no power in this place, there will be perfection in everything in heaven. And the most important and only way to get to heaven is to accept Jesus as our Lord and savior and there is no other short cut in order for us to make heaven, John 3:16 says,

"For God so loved the world, that he gave his only begotten Son, that whosoever believeth in him should not perish but have everlasting life."

The Name of Jesus

Introduction

Jesus is the Greek form of Joshua, the name Jesus means "Savior" it is the same name as Joshua in the Old Testament; it is given to our Lord because "He saves His people from their sins and this is His special role." He saves them from the guilt of sin, by cleansing them in His own atoning blood. He saves them from the dominion of sin by putting in their hearts the sanctifying spirit. He saves them from the presence of sin, when He takes them out of this world to rest with Him. He will save them from all the consequences of sin, when He shall give them a glorious body on the last day. This name is a name above all other names in earth and in heaven.

Why am I writing a chapter on the Name of Jesus Christ, as we can see names are very significant both in the bible days and also in the present day, and a name is what identifies a person. A name goes further as an identity. The greatest name and sweetest name of all is Jesus, His name is an index to his calling but also his power, we need to see how faith joined to his name can bring salvation and healing.

Explanation of the Name Lord Jesus Christ

Lord: refers to Jesus being God, it is bringing all that was true of Yahweh to the person of Jesus, this is essential to our profession of faith and affirmation that Jesus is Lord. If a believer confesses that "Jesus is Lord" and believes in his or her heart that God raised him from the dead, the same will be saved" (Rom 10:9)

The word "Christ" refers to Jesus being Messiah, Messiah and Christ can be used interchangeably, Messiah means the anointed one, anointed is the Greek equivalent of Messiah, and it was the long expected fulfillment of the Old Testament prophecies. Lord Jesus Christ embodies three things in the title.

Jesus: the human name

Lord: the Deity of Jesus

Christ: His being the Jews Messiah or anointed one

Jesus had no earthly father, Joseph and Mary had no sexual relations in the supernatural conception of Jesus (Matt 1:25.) Mary, the mother of Jesus, was a virgin who became pregnant by the divine visitation of the Holy Spirit. Hence, Jesus was literally God's own Son (John 3:16, 1:18) for the fulfillment of the God-head lived in Jesus.

Different Names of Jesus

1. The Son of David (Matt 22:41-42)
2. The Son of God (John 3:16)
3. Savior (Luke 2:11)
4. Lamb of God (John 1:29)
5. Mediator (Galatians 3:19)
6. Lord of glory (1 Corinthians 2:8)

7. King of Kings, Lord of Lords (Rev. 19:16)

8. Prophet (Mathew 21:11)

9. Priest (Heb. 4:14)

10. King (1 Timothy 1:17)

Other Names of Christ

1. ADVOCATE: 1 John 2:1 "My little children, these things write I unto you, that ye sin not. And if any man sin, we have an advocate with the Father, Jesus Christ the righteous."

2. ADAM: 1 Corinthians 15:45 "And so it is written, the first man Adam was made a living soul; the last Adam was made a quickening spirit."

3. ALMIGHTY: Revelation 1:8 "I am Alpha and Omega, the beginning and the ending, saith the Lord, which is, and which was, and which is to come, the Almighty."

4. ALPHA AND OMEGA: Revelation 1:8 "I am Alpha and Omega, the beginning and the ending, saith the Lord, which is, and which was, and which is to come, the Almighty."

5. APOSTLE OF OUR PROFESSION: Hebrews 3:1 "Wherefore, holy brethren, partakers of the heavenly calling, consider the Apostle and High Priest of our profession, Christ Jesus."

6. ARM OF THE LORD: Isaiah 51:9 "Awake, awake, put on strength, O arm of the LORD; awake, as in the ancient days, in the generations of old. Art thou not it that hath cut Rahab, and wounded the dragon?"

7. AUTHOR AND FINISHER OF OUR FAITH: Hebrews 12:2 "Looking unto Jesus the author and

finisher of our faith; who for the joy that was set before him endured the cross, despising the shame, and is set down at the right hand of the throne of God."

8. AUTHOR OF ETERNAL SALVATION: Hebrews 5:9 "And being made perfect, he became the author of eternal salvation unto all them that obey him."

9. BELOVED SON: Matthew 12:18 "Behold my servant, whom I have chosen; my beloved, in whom my soul is well pleased: I will put my spirit upon him, and he shall show judgment to the Gentiles."

10. BREAD OF LIFE: John 6:32 "Then Jesus said unto them, Verily, verily, I say unto you, Moses gave you not that bread from heaven; but my Father giveth you the true bread from heaven."

11. CAPTAIN OF SALVATION: Hebrews 2:10 " For it became him, for whom are all things, and by whom are all things, in bringing many sons unto glory, to make the captain of their salvation perfect through sufferings."

12. CONSOLATION OF ISRAEL: Luke 2:25 "And, behold, there was a man in Jerusalem, whose name was Simeon; and the same man was just and devout, waiting for the consolation of Israel: and the Holy Ghost was upon him."

13. COUNSELOR: Isaiah 9:6 "For unto us a child is born, unto us a son is given: and the government shall be upon his shoulder: and his name shall be called Wonderful, Counselor, The mighty God, The everlasting Father, and The Prince of Peace."

14. DELIVERER: Romans 11:26 "And so all Israel shall be saved: as it is written, there shall come out of Zion the Deliverer, and shall turn away ungodliness from Jacob."

15. EVERLASTING FATHER: Isaiah 9:6 "For unto us a child is born, unto us a son is given: and the government shall be upon his shoulder: and his name shall be called Wonderful, Counselor, The mighty God, The everlasting Father, The Prince of Peace."

16. FIRST AND LAST: Revelation 1:17 "And when I saw him, I fell at his feet as dead. And he laid his right hand upon me, saying unto me, Fear not; I am the first and the last."

17. FORERUNNER: Hebrews 6:20 "Whither the forerunner is for us entered, even Jesus, made an high priest for ever after the order of Melchisedec."

18. GREAT HIGH PRIEST: Hebrews 4:14 "Seeing then that we have a great high priest, that is passed into the heavens, Jesus the Son of God, let us hold fast our profession."

19. HOLY ONE OF ISRAEL: Isaiah 41:14 "Fear not, thou worm Jacob, and ye men of Israel; I will help thee, saith the LORD, and thy redeemer, the Holy One of Israel."

20. IMAGE OF GOD: 2 Corinthians 4:4 "In whom the god of this world hath blinded the minds of them which believe not, lest the light of the glorious gospel of Christ, who is the image of God, should shine unto them."

21. LEADER AND COMMANDER: Isaiah 55:4 "Behold, I have given him for a witness to the people, a leader and commander to the people."

22. LIGHT OF THE WORLD: John 8:12 "Then spake Jesus again unto them, saying, I am the light of the world: he that followeth me shall not walk in darkness, but shall have the light of life."

23. LORD OF OUR RIGHTEOUSNESS: Jeremiah 23:6 "In his days Judah shall be saved, and Israel shall dwell safely: and this is his name whereby he shall be called, THE LORD OUR RIGHTEOUSNESS."

24. MESSENGER OF THE COVENANT: Malachi 3:1 "Behold, I will send my messenger, and he shall prepare the way before me: and the Lord, whom ye seek, shall suddenly come to his temple, even the messenger of the covenant, whom ye delight in: behold, he shall come, saith the LORD of hosts."

25. MORNING STAR: Revelation 22:16 "I Jesus have sent mine angel to testify unto you these things in the churches. I am the root and the offspring of David, and the bright and morning star."

26. PRINCE OF KINGS: Revelation 1:5 "And from Jesus Christ, who is the faithful witness, and the first begotten of the dead, and the prince of the kings of the earth. Unto him that loved us, and washed us from our sins in his own blood."

27. PRINCE OF PEACE: Isaiah 9:6 "For unto us a child is born, unto us a son is given: and the government shall be upon his shoulder: and his name shall be called Wonderful, Counselor, The mighty God, The everlasting Father, The Prince of Peace."

28. PROPHET: Luke 24:19 "And he said unto them, what things? And they said unto him, Concerning Jesus of Nazareth, which was a prophet mighty in deed and word before God and all the people."

29. RESURRECTION AND LIFE: John 11:25 "Jesus said unto her, I am the resurrection, and the life: he that believeth in me, though he were dead, yet shall he live."

30. SHEPHERD AND BISHOP OF SOULS: 1 Peter 2:25 "For ye were as sheep going astray; but are now returned unto the Shepherd and Bishop of your souls."

All these names and many more are the names of Jesus known, all because of his awesomeness and also because of who His father is. The sound of the name of Jesus gives us instant access to the father, because "Jesus is the way the truth and the life. No one comes to the Father except through Him".

And salvation is found in no one else, for there is no other name under heaven given to men by which we must be saved" (Rom 10:13), the name of Jesus gets the fathers attention, that name therefore must be uttered- confessing with your mouth "Jesus is Lord".

The Effects of the Name of Jesus

1. What the sound of the name of Jesus does to Satan: Satan is real. He is a fallen angel (Revs 12:7) bent on seducing us, destroying us, and leading us to hell. Although we humans are very weak and stupid compared to Satan, we have authority over him by the power of Jesus (Mt 10:1). In fact, Jesus has already irreversibly defeated Satan. "The strife is over, the battle done." All that remains is to place Jesus' enemies beneath His feet (Heb 10:13).

2. What the sound of the name of Jesus does to Sinners: The name of Jesus embodies all to sinners, Jesus have not come to call the righteous, but sinners (Matt 9:13), and it is not the healthy who needs a doctor, but the sick (Luke 5:31). For I delivered unto you first of all that which I also received, how that Christ died for our sins according to the Scriptures; And that He was buried, and that He rose again the third day according to the Scriptures(1Cor 15: 3,4).

The name of Jesus cleanses the sinner, and makes them whole and brand new.

3. What the name of Jesus does to the poor: The name of Jesus is so powerful that it gives the poor confidence and makes them have hope: Acts 3:6 "Then Peter said, Silver and gold have I none; but such as I have I give you: In the name of Jesus Christ of Nazareth rise up and walk" that's what the name of Jesus does. The man at the gate was expecting money from peter, because he was lame and also a beggar, but instead of giving him money, peter used the name of Jesus to heal him.

There is tremendous power in the name of Jesus, everything we go through in life we can count on this name with faith, to bring us out of any situation that we find ourselves.

Conclusion

There is only one God in existence and He is Jesus Christ. He became a human in order to die for us. This gives Him the right to forgive our sins. He will do that if you want your sins forgiven and you are sorry for your sins. And after we are born again the name of Jesus is required for all effective believing prayer to the father in heaven, and any prayer in the name of Jesus is therefore the means for accomplishing on the part of the Christian and on the part of God what would not otherwise have been accomplished. It is the highest work of every Christian; it enters into the loftiest privilege; it is the key to every spiritual treasure. The devil is afraid of the name of Jesus. And as it is stated in Philippians 2:10,

> *"That at the name of Jesus every knee should bow, of things in heaven, and the things in earth, and things under earth."*

The Jealousy of God

Introduction

Why is God a Jealous God? It is important to understand how the word "Jealousy" is used, when we human beings use the word jealousy we use it in the sense of being envious of a person who has something we don't have. One might be jealous or envious of another person because he or she has a nice car or home (possessions) or a person might be jealous or envious of another person because of some ability or skill that other person has (such as athletic ability). Another example would be that one person might be jealous or envious of another because of his or her beauty or personality.

In Exodus 20:5, it is not that God is jealous or envious because someone has something He wants or needs. Exodus 20:4-5 says

> *"Thou shalt not make unto thee any graven image, or any likeness of anything that is in the heaven above, or that is beneath or that is in*

*the water under the earth, thou shalt not bow
down thyself to them or serve them: for I the
Lord thy God am a jealous God.....''*

Notice that God is jealous when someone gives another,
something that rightly belongs to Him.

Glory of His Name is at Stake

God actually said: His name is Jealous (Ex. 34:14), so it is
the glory of His name that is at stake, therefore when people
who are called by his name (2 Chron. 7:14) go off the rails,
disobey Him, look toward the world or flirt with any of God's
competitors, God is always angry and will show it because the
glory of His name is at stake. Ancient Israel sadly turned to
the worship of idols which was visible, when they got tired of
having to wait on the invisible God. When the people saw that
Moses was so long in coming down from the mountain, they
gathered around Aaron and said:

*"Come, make us gods who will go before us.
As for this fellow Moses brought us up out of
Egypt, we don't Know what happened to him",
then Aaron wanting to validate himself for going with the people, said, "so I told them, Whosoever has any gold jewelry, take it off", Then
they gave me the gold, and I threw it into the
fire, and out came this calf" (Ex 32:34).*

God rose up so many prophets, prophets who exposed and
warned against any kind of Idolatry, like the one we saw in the
last paragraph.

God raised up Elijah when King Ahab allowed the prophets
of Baal to flourish, and also during Jeremiahs day, he proph-

esied that Jerusalem would be shattered and the people taken captive to Babylon.

How Do We Make God Jealous?

Avariciousness or Covetousness which is idolatry: what does idolatry look like today? It is the activity of the human heart. This is not a deed of the body that follows a fruit on a branch. It starts in the heart, craving, wanting, enjoying being satisfied by anything that you treasure more than God, that is an idol, and that is exactly what makes God Jealous. Avariciousness a disordered love or desire, loving more than God what ought to be loved less than God and only for the sake of God. But covetousness is the condition that this disordered heart is into, an act of loving too much what ought to be loved less, and that is why the wrath of God is coming. That is what idolatry looks like today and it is everywhere in our culture.

In Romans 1:25,

"They exchange the truth about God for a lie and worshipped and served the creature."

Anything that is created rather than the creator, and note that there is no wrath for the children of God, and why is that? Because in 1 Thessalonians 1:10, you turned to God from idols to serve the living and true God and to wait for his Son from heaven whom he raised from dead, Jesus who delivers us from the wrath to come. So when we turn to Christ from idols we escape the wrath of God because He is for us. God is for us in Christ on the Cross.

God's Jealousy is His Holy Love for Us

The jealous Holy Spirit lives in us. Although he can be grieved, he nonetheless brings us back to himself when we slip. Were it not for this reason, we will never come back, and this explains God's chastening, or discipline (Heb 12: 5-11).

The Principles of Gods Chastening are as Follows:

Every Christian will be disciplined, Heb 12:6-10,

> *"For whom the lord loveth, He chasteneth, and courageth every son whom he receiveth, if he endure chastening, God dealeth with you as with sons, for what son is he whom the father chasteneth not, But if ye be without chastisement, wherefore all are partakers, then ye are bastards and not sons, furthermore we have had fathers of our flesh which corrected us, and we gave them reverence: shall we not much rather be in subjection unto the father of spirits and live? For they verily for a few days chastened us after their own pleasure, but he for our profit that we might be partakers of his holiness".*

Being disciplined is painful, Heb 12:11,

> *"Now no chastening for the present seemeth to be joyous, but grievous: nevertheless afterward it yieldeth the peaceable fruit of righteousness unto them which are exercised thereby."*

It is to lead us to holiness Heb 12:10-11, and it is because God is Jealous that he chastens. There are so many people in the bible that learned that, Jonah learned this (Jonah 2), and David learned this in (2 Sam. 12).

Conclusion

As we know that jealousy as a human attribute is unattractive, but God was totally open about His jealousy, starting right from time, even in the Ten Commandments etc. God is jealous for his glory, if we as Christians attribute glory to anyone or anything other than the triune God, we make the person or object an idol, and this makes God jealous and provokes him to anger. God wants total control of our lives, because He shed his blood on the cross for our sins. We should always be subject to his authority and respect Him with our lives, in order to avoid Gods Jealousy. Every day in our busy lives we should always know that God is a jealous God, Ex 34:14,

"I, the Lord your God, am a jealous God."

Once we always remember this we will not be building or worshiping different idols (Money, fancy things, people etc) other than God.

Temptation

Introduction

This is a very insightful chapter, because we have all been tempted before, including you, the reader. Temptation is that which moves us to sin, and we are tempted because of different things like our lusts, possessions, money, lack of self-examination, boastfulness and pride etc, and I believe also that when we are tempted and fall into it, we lose our fellowship with God, we lose the joy of our salvation and we lose the reward in heaven. And also note that one can be tempted and the person will surmount the temptation and not commit any sin. From the onset of the bible starting with Adam and Eve, the serpent did tempt Eve and she fell and committed sin, by eating the forbidden fruit (Genesis 3:2-14).

The Architect of Our Temptation?

From this chapter, it is evident that God is the architect of the situation that lies behind our being tempted. He does not do the tempting, but He tests us by letting us be tempted, and just allows the temptation to happen, and he does this to see our faith and trust in him, a typical example In the bible is Job. God allowed Satan to tempt Job according to Job 1:9-12,

"Then Satan answered the Lord, and said doth Job fear God nought?, hast not thou made a hedge about him and about his house, and about all that he hath on every side?, thou hast blessed the work of his hands and his substance is increased in the land, but put forth thine hand now, and touch all he hath, and he will curse thee to thy face, and the Lord said unto Satan, behold all that he hath is in thy power, only upon himself put not forth thine hand, so Satan went forth from the presence of the Lord".

From this passage we can see clearly that God allowed Satan to tempt Job to see and prove how much faith he has in the Lord. So when we are being tempted we should always have our faith and trust in the Lord, so we can overcome. James 1:2-3,

"My brethren, count it all joy when ye fall into divers temptations, knowing this, that the trying of your faith worketh patience".

As I stated earlier, God permits the temptation as we have already seen with Job, a typical example from the bible, God creates a situation that lets us see how strong we are, note God does not directly tempt us but the situation He brings about is His test for us, and this is done by Him to see how faithful and obedient we are to him.

As believers, we should never tempt God, but sometimes we see ourselves tempting God, even as the Devil tempted Jesus. we as Christians sometimes tempt God in different ways by challenging his power. Since God can do all things, we think sometimes by being angry at God, we can move him to do something on our behalf, and by deliberately walking into temptation etc. and when we do all these things, we should note that God has already warned us as seen in Matt 4:6:

> *"And saith unto him, if thou be the Son of God, cast thyself down: for it is written, He shall give his angels charge concerning thee: and in their hands they shall bear thee up, lest at any time thou dash thy foot against a stone. And Jesus said unto him, it is written again Thou shalt not tempt the Lord thy God."*

From this passage we can clearly see that we should not tempt God in any way. Example we cannot see a poison, and knowing fully well of its poisonous potency, proceed to drink it and say that our God will save us, it won't work.

Temptation Types

When we are tempted, it always ends in one of two ways: we either resist the temptation or yield to it. We either move away from the temptation or allow it to swallow us. Any person that has resisted the temptation has the feeling of freedom that the particular decision brings. On the other hand, anyone that yields to the tempter knows the feeling of emptiness that follows and the pain it causes. I believe that everything we do in life can be a basis for our temptation. Take for example food; we can be tempted to over eat. Other common areas of temptation include: sex, pride, ambition, jealousy, gossip, slander, unforgiving spirit, need for prestige, hatred etc. We should be prayerful all the time whenever we see ourselves in temptation, we must retrace our steps and look unto our God the author and finisher of our faith. We will most definitely come out victorious and we will definitely excel and overcome in Jesus name. As mentioned in the list above, we can see that temptation arises through our daily encounters; it deals with things we are involved in everyday, and it is stated clearly that temptations always come through our weakness, and we should always know that the devil can only go as far as God allows him to.

Resisting Temptation

We should always know that regardless of the situation we find ourselves in, God is able to see us through, if we have absolute trust in him. As believers, it is important that we always watch and pray, because the devil is always seeking for opportunities to severe our relationship with God. It should be noted that any temptation can be resisted, we only need to know our weaknesses and ask God to strengthen those weaknesses and also avoid areas or things that are susceptible to our weaknesses. For example, a man cannot be in a room filled with naked women and say to himself, I will not fall into temptation, the best thing to do at that situation is to walk out, and not fall into temptation. We should be wise children of God to know when we are being tempted, and we should always bear in our minds that temptation is like a rattle snake; once we fall into it, we might not come out of it, and we may also die from the poison.

Conclusion

God is at the center of all situations and circumstances (temptation) from the beginning to the end of our lives, God is a master planner and supreme architect. Who can measure unto him? From this chapter we can all see that God does not tempt us, but he allows Satan to tempt us to see were our faith is. An example we saw is of Job a man of timeless importance and wonder, a man of God with impeccable credentials, who faced temptation with a tidal wave of live challenges and struggles, as we all know he possessed extreme wealth, influence, integrity, character, compassion, he became a man that lost everything but through all this temptation Job never cursed God or disobeyed him. This is exactly how God wants our faith to be because everything we have is Gods' and no temptation is able to cross our paths without God's knowledge and permission. Hence every temptation we go through can be resisted; however, and we should always implement the strategy of resisting temptation which include: watching and praying, avoiding situations in which we know we are likely to be tempted, and we should always think about how God will look at us when we give into temptation and we should bear in mind that we will always lose a lot when we give into temptation, we will lose our fellowship with God, the joy of our salvation and most importantly our reward in Heaven.

The Gift of Wisdom

Introduction

Wisdom is the ability to see in advance what the right cause of action is. God's gift of wisdom always includes his impartation of Godly wisdom, which cannot be fully discussed without the mention of King Solomon. God told Solomon to request anything of him, guaranteeing that he will do whatever is asked. Solomon never asked for riches or fame, rather he asked God to give him the gift of wisdom. God was so impressed by Solomon's request that he not only gave him wisdom, but also added riches and fame. Solomon's wisdom was evident in his first judgment in Israel.

> *"Unto man he said behold, the fear of the Lord, that is the wisdom and to depart from evil is understanding."*

This exactly means what it is saying clearly, the fear of the Lord is the beginning of wisdom, there is nothing a mortal man can do without wisdom, and true wisdom comes from God.

*"Get wisdom and understanding, forget it not,
neither decline from words of thy mouth."
Prov. 4:5*

And in verse 7 it says,

*"Wisdom is the principal thing, therefore get
wisdom and with all thy getting get understanding."*

Before I move any further I will look at the major difference between wisdom and knowledge.

Difference Between Wisdom and Knowledge

Wisdom and knowledge are recurring themes in the Bible. Both are related but not synonymous. The dictionary defines wisdom as "the ability to discern or judge what is true, right, or lasting." Knowledge, on the other hand, is "information gained through experience, reasoning, or acquaintance." Knowledge can exist without wisdom, but not the other way around. One can be knowledgeable without being wise. Knowledge is knowing how to use a gun; wisdom is knowing when to use it and when to keep it holstered. God wants us to have knowledge of Him and what He expects of us. In order to obey Him, we have to have knowledge of the commands. But as equally important as having knowledge is having wisdom. Knowing facts about God and the Bible is not all there is to wisdom. Wisdom is a gift from God.

*"If any of you lacks wisdom, you should ask
God, who gives generously to all without finding fault, and it will be given to you." James 1:5.*

God blesses us with wisdom in order for us to glorify Him and use the knowledge we have of Him. The best place in the Bible to learn of biblical wisdom is the book of Proverbs. It speaks of both biblical knowledge and wisdom: "The fear of the LORD is the beginning of knowledge, but fools despise wisdom and instruction." To start on the path to knowledge is to fear the Lord, and God can then begin to provide us with wisdom through Christ, who the Bible says is wisdom itself:

> *1 Corinthians 1:30, "It is because of him that you are in Christ Jesus, who has become for us wisdom from God that is, our righteousness, holiness and redemption".*

Wisdom is also both vertical and horizontal. Vertical towards God, to know his ways and horizontal towards others to show selfless concern.

Knowledge is what is gathered over time through study of the Scriptures. It can be said that wisdom, in turn, acts properly upon that knowledge. Wisdom is the fitting application of knowledge. Knowledge understands the light has turned red; wisdom applies the brakes. Knowledge sees the quicksand; wisdom walks around it. Knowledge memorizes the Ten Commandments; wisdom obeys them. Knowledge learns of God; wisdom loves Him.

Therefore, the gift of wisdom is very important in our lives; we should also know and note that wisdom is very possible to be received when we ask it of the Lord as seen in James 1:5.

> *"If any of you lack wisdom let him ask of God, that giveth to all men liberally" and in verse 7 "But let him ask in faith, nothing wavering for that wavereth is like a wave of the sea, driven with the wind and tossed."*

This bible passage is telling me when asking for wisdom, ask for it with unshakable faith. And there are so many attributes and characteristics of the gift of wisdom, which I will be explaining in the next paragraph.

Characteristics of the Gift of Wisdom with Bible Verse

1. **Guidance:** Proverbs 3:5-6

Trust in the Lord with all your heart and lean not on your own understanding;

in all your ways acknowledge him,

and he will make your paths straight.

This might be the most quoted passage in all of Proverbs; maybe you've memorized it. But wherever you're headed in life, these words will always remind you who directs your steps.

2. **Discernment:** Proverbs 14:12

There is a way that seems right to a man,

but in the end it leads to death.

Yeah, that verse ends on kind of a downer. But you get the point: Sometimes something seems right, but it might be the wrong choice after all. That's why we've always got to ask God to help us make wise decisions.

3. **Confidence:** Proverbs 3:25-26

Have no fear of sudden disaster

or of the ruin that overtakes the wicked,

for the Lord will be your confidence

and will keep your foot from being snared.

Finishing high school, college, can be kind of scary. You might not feel as confident as you did before. But remember: "The Lord will be your confidence."

4. Work: Proverbs 6:6-9

Go to the ant, you sluggard;

consider its ways and be wise!

It has no commander, no overseer or ruler,

yet it stores its provisions in summer

and gathers its food at harvest.

How long will you lie there, you sluggard?

When will you get up from your sleep?

Life lessons from an ant? Yep. Ants might be the hardest-working critters alive. They're always busy, always planning ahead. Being on your own—whether in college or at a full-time job—is hard work. It's tempting to get lazy—especially in college, where it's easy to sleep through those early-morning classes. Mom won't be there to tell you, for the 13th time, to get out of bed; there will be "no commander, no overseer or ruler." You'll have to kick yourself into gear, because nobody else will do it for you.

5. Relationships: Proverbs 12:26

A righteous man is cautious in friendship,

but the way of the wicked leads them astray.

Here's a great verse on choosing friends wisely. As you begin to develop new friendships after high school, college ask God to point you to people who won't lead you astray.

6. Sexual purity: Prov. 6:25-26, 28

Do not lust in your heart after her beauty

or let her captivate you with her eyes,

for the prostitute reduces you to a loaf of bread,

and the adulteress preys upon your very life. ...

Can a man walk on hot coals

without his feet being scorched?

You might be saying, "Prostitutes and adultery? That doesn't apply to me." But these verses are about much more than that. They're about the strong temptation of sex, a temptation that affects us all. This passage clearly says sex outside of marriage is also outside of God's perfect plan. When we violate that plan, we walk "on hot coals"—and get burned.

7. Money: Proverbs 11:28

Whoever trusts in riches will fall,

but the righteous will thrive like a green leaf.

Whether you're off to college or a job, it's easy to think that money will bring happiness or solve your problems. But the Bible is clear that money doesn't do those things. If you want to "thrive like a green leaf," pursue righteousness, not riches.

8. Parents: Proverbs 23:22, 25

Listen to your father, who gave you life,

and do not despise your mother when she is old. ...

May your father and mother be glad;

may she who gave you birth rejoice!

It's perfectly natural to want independence—and, ultimately, to break away from Mom and Dad. But don't rush that process. Even when you're on your own, your parents are still your parents and deserve your respect. Do what you can to make them proud and glad you're their child.

9. Compassion: Proverbs 19:17

He who is kind to the poor lends to the Lord,

and he will reward him for what he has done.

We all tend to get so caught up in our own lives that we sometimes forget there are hurting people all around us. But God always wants us to share his great love with others. Volunteer with a local ministry. Take a short-term missions trip. Make time to reach out and touch someone.

10. The future: Proverbs 23:18

There is surely a future hope for you,

and your hope will not be cut off.

You're probably wondering what your future holds. But this verse says you don't have to worry about it: If you follow God, he'll take care of it—and he'll take care of you. Nothing can cut you off from his love. He will carry you through, all the way.

Conclusion

Wisdom and knowledge are very important in our everyday life, and towards Christ and the church. Without the gift of wisdom, we cannot achieve anything in our personal life. The scripture encourages us to recognize our need for the gift of wisdom and ask God for it, and as we stated earlier in this chapter, wisdom operates in two directions vertically towards God, as we seek to know His ways and horizontally towards others, as we exercise it in our relationships and dealings. Prov. 9:10: "The fear of the Lord is the beginning of wisdom and the knowledge of the Holy understanding" Fearing the Lord is basically this: you recognize that He is the Creator, your Master, the Lord of all; He's holy and awesome and calls the shots. And in response you willingly submit yourself to Him and His plan for your life. Without this, there is no wisdom. It starts with salvation. It continues in reverent humility. And the best way to gain the ultimate wisdom in our life is to repudiate our own wisdom and take instead the infinite wisdom of God... God has charged Himself with full responsibility for our eternal happiness and stands ready to take over the management of our lives the moment we turn in faith to Him.

Man, Sin &
Salvation

In this chapter, Man, Sin and Salvation is a three part work and an in-depth chapter, it is deep because it deals with the core of creation of man from the beginning of the bible from Genesis 1:27,

> "So God created man in his own image, the image of God created he him, Male and female created he them" KJV.

So this Chapter will explore more on the creation of man, Sin, the origin of sin, which is how the Serpent deceived Adam and Eve to eating the fruit from Genesis 3:1-24, Lucifer (the fallen angel) and how sin affects a Christian, in the world today, and we will also find out that sin is a power that enslaves a Christian in the world today, it puts us in bondage, and we will see that sin is much more than violation of a taboo or the transgression of an external ordinance. It signifies the rupture of a personal relationship with God, a betrayal of the trust He placed in us. We become most aware of our sinfulness in the presence of the holy spirit, Isaiah 6:5, Luke 5:8 and through this chapter we will see that we can be freed from this power by encountering God through reading the word of God, The Bible, dwelling on it constantly, praying and worshipping God daily. After that we will look at salvation, which is only through Jesus Christ, "for God so loved the world that he gave his only begotten Son, that whosoever believeth in him should not perish, but have everlasting life. God is the way the truth and salvation. No one can make it to heaven only through Jesus, and we will look into the numerous factors that are involved in our Salvation including faith, repentance, confess the blood of Christ, the gospel, grace and baptism.

MAN

From the dictionary definition, man is a member of the Homo sapiens specie or all the members of this species collectively, without regards to sex. This is worldly definition of man, but we should note that man is created by God in Genesis 1:26-27,

> "And God said let us make man in our image, after our likeness: and let them have dominion over the fish of the sea, and over the fowl of the air, and over the cattle. And over all the earth and over every creeping thing that creepeth upon the earth. So God created man in his own image, the image of God created he him."

And man has most of the qualities of God because God created man in his own image. God created man for man to worship Him, and man had pure fellowship with God. And also God gave man the freewill to choose to eat any fruit which they want to eat from the garden And the lord commanded in Genesis 2:16-17,

"You are free to eat from any tree in the garden, but you must not eat from the tree of the knowledge of good and evil, for when you eat of it you will surely die."

So many Christians find themselves somewhere between a conservative and a broad chronology for mans' origin. Yet in spite of individual preference, one must give assent to God's creative work in producing man in order to think biblically about humanity. The essence of faith begins in the words "I believe in God the Father Almighty, creator of heaven and earth." Man is not only Gods creation but the pinnacle of his creative effort. Long before modern precision in such things, the ancients were aware of human beings, anatomical similarities with members of the animal kingdom, but despite these similarities, the biblical viewpoint was never to confuse humans with animals. Human beings are distinct, the high point of Gods creative work, the apex of his handicraft. The progression of the created things in Genesis 1 is climactic, all of Gods created work culminated in his fashioning of human beings.

Sociologically, the distinct behavior characteristics of man include language, tool making and culture. Distinct experiential characteristics include reflective awareness, ethical concern, aesthetic urges, historical awareness and metaphysical concern. These factors individually and collectively separate humans from other forms of animate life. Man is far more than the "naked ape" of some modern evolutionary theories. But sociology alone does not suffice to explain the full nature of humankind. Man bears a continuity with God's creation (assumed in the word of Genesis 2:7, being fashioned from dust of the ground), man being also distinct from all that preceded them, as it was into a new creature that God breathed the breath of life so that he became a living being. The wording of the text deals a blow to the theory of gradualism in man's development. It was not into one of the developing creatures that God gave an extra boost or a distinctive nature but into a fully fashioned yet inanimate creature that he breathed the breath of life. The animating principles of humanity come directly as a gift from God. Man was created by God as Male and Female (Genesis 1:27) meaning that what is said generally of Man must be said to be both male and female, and the truest picture of what it means to be human is to be found in the context of man and woman together. The commands to multiply and exercise sovereignty over the earth were given to both sexes as shared responsibility. Similarly, it is both male and female that have rebelled against God and bear the consequences of that primeval sin in the post-fall world, and both male and female that Christ came to redeem (Galatians 3:28) at the same time the words male and female denote true distinctions. Many perceived gender differences may be culturally conditioned, yet the prime sexual distinction between male and female are divinely intended.

The Natural Man

The biblical view of humanity begins in the assertion that man is a person made up physical and nonphysical properties, a person is "a bodily soul" there is no person in the body only nor can one easily think of a bodiless spirit as a person, a purely material, physical view of humanity is frightfully deficient, at the same time an overemphasis on the spirit and a de emphasis on the physical is neither realistic nor balanced. One might say I am a person whose existence is presently very dependent upon my physical body. But I am more than a body, more than flesh, when my body dies, I still live. When my flesh decays, I exist. But one day I shall live in a body again. For the notion of a disembodied spirit is not a full measure of humanity. God's deal for me is to live my life in my new body, so hope of eternal state, I believe in the resurrection of the body and life everlasting.

One cannot go far in thinking of the nature of man from the biblical vantage point without facing the problem of the fall. Genesis 3 suggests that unfallen humans were immortal, that their powers of sexual reproduction were not originally bound in the pain of childbearing and that their work was not troubled by reversals in nature. After the fall, however, all was changed within each person, between the male and female, in their interaction with nature, and their relationship with the creator. As a result of the fall of man it has become profoundly fallen, and thus extending to every part of the person. The term total depravity need not mean that one is as evil as he or she might be, at the same time, Gods image in human beings continues in some way after the fall, providing the divine rationale for salvation. It is essential because of Gods estimation of the intrinsic worth of humanity that the divine justification of salvation may be maintained.

Man was created good by God, but has become evil by his own devices, and yet in God's power may recapture the good again. The rediscovery of what it means to be fully human as God's shadow is found in the life of Jesus, whose human life is the new beginning for humanity. Hence, Jesus is the new Adam in his model a new beginning that replaces the former pattern.

Man's Eternal Destiny

"It is appointed for man to die once, and after that comes judgment" Hebrews 9:27.

Is Heaven real? Is Hell real? Is there eternal life? Without man asking questions there will not be answers and man will not have purpose. Birth and death are the inseparable confines of all life on earth. Death is a great discloser of what is in a man, our life dreams for the perfect world and endless search for truth, death achieves the ideal, now no man would dispute that all men die sooner or later. We also know that the bible plainly speaks of a great day of judgment coming upon the world. The appointment of death is for "the cause or reason" that is sin, in order words physical death is a consequence of sin, the Bible states that:

*"By the sweat of your brow you will eat your
food until you return to the ground, since from
it you were taken, for dust you are and to dust
you will return." Genesis 3:19*

Death proves the universality of sin.

*"Therefore, just as through one man sin entered
into the world, and death through sin, and so
death spread to all men, because all sinned."
Romans 6:23*

This explains the whole of it. The wages of sin is death; this
is one of the saddest, but profound truth of the world. Sin is a
master of his servants and pays wages which is "death." Tem-
poral, Spiritual and eternal are due wages of sin. But eternal
life is the gift of God. The difference is remarkable. Evil works,
merit the reward they receive, good works do not. The former
demand wages, the latter accepts a free gift. But the gift of God
is eternal life.

God gives to those who turn from sin, life eternal. It is his
gracious gift, conditioned on refusing to be a slave to sin, and
embracing the unmerited grace given through Jesus Christ
our lord. The gift of God is eternal life. And the gift is through
Jesus Christ our Lord. Christ purchased it, prepared us for it,
preserves us to it, Christ is our all. All physical death ends in
resurrection of the body as seen in Job 19:25. Physical death
affects the body only and is neither a cessation of life nor
reincarnation. Physical death has for the believer a peculiar
qualification. It is called "to be at home with the Lord" because
his body may be "raised in glory" at any moment. At the believer's death he is "clothed upon" with a "house from heaven"
pending the resurrection of the earthly house" and is at once
with the Lord. Death is bound to happen to all for the Bible
said: "it is appointed unto men"—to all mankind, it is not an

appointment for one, but for all. Immediately after death, we shall pass into the eternal world, and then every being's eternal destination will be made known. This seems necessarily implied in the supposition that we may continue to reign in glory with our Lord, or be cast to eternal damnation and be miserable.

Every single day about 80,000 people die on earth. In another 90 years, nearly everyone who is on earth today will be gone. It can happen at any time, at anywhere, to anybody. Some people logically seek this and ask whether science has done a sufficient job in explaining the theories of life and death. Based on my opinion and with the backing of scriptures, science cannot explain life and death in any way, but life and death is in the hands of God Almighty, the Maker of heaven and earth. We now look at Sin, and what is sin; how was it introduced and what impact does it have upon our lives as believers? How can Christians strive to live a sin free life?

THE GENESIS OF SIN

What is Sin? Sin is simply defined as doing what is wrong or not doing what is right according to God's rules 1 john 3:4 if God says "do not lie" and you lie, then you have sinned. If God says "do not steal" and you steal, then you have sinned. According to God, sin separates us from him Isaiah 59:2. The first Sin ever recorded in the bible is the sin of disobedience, which was recorded in Gen 3:1-10, and it was when Adam and Eve disobeyed God by eating the fruit in the middle of the Garden of Eden, sin in its original form and to this day is Insubordination. It is rebellion against God's revealed truth and will. As we have seen it in the bible and in real life. I must point out that sin is not only reserved for those who do not know Christ, but unfortunately it is something that is rampant in Christ's church. Paul says,

> *"For the good that I will to do, I do not do, but
> the evil I will not to do, that I practice. Now if I*

do what I will not to do, it is no longer I who do
it, but sin that dwells in me." (Romans 7:19-20)

Sin is the devil's influence that has been planted in our hearts and that separates us from God, causing us to rebel against him.

The scriptures are packed full of instances of rebellion of the creatures (which represents "us") against the creator (GOD). The person that introduced sin to the world is Lucifer, a ranking member of the angelic host, who rebelled against God and was cast down from heaven into the pits of hell together with one-third of the angels. Lucifer's sin is recorded in Isaiah 14:13 where he said,

"I will ascend into heaven, I will exalt my
throne above the stars of God, I will also sit on
the mount of the congregation on the farthest
sides."

Lucifer was actually an exalted angel of God. In fact his name is translated as the morning star but clearly, he harbored feelings of envy and resentment towards God and the Son especially, since Gods beloved Son was placed above all of the angels, even over this apparent agent of God, Lucifer. As the angels bowed before God and his Son Jesus, Lucifer would do so also, but in his heart he deceived himself into thinking that he could be greater than God and that he deserved the exalted position that Jesus had received. Lucifer clearly was not God all though he thought he could be. He was not omnipresent, being in every place, omniscient knowing all things, omnipotent being all powerful. He was merely a created being just as you and I. remember in the days of Job when we are told that Satan came before God and how God allowed the devil to afflict Job, because he claimed that Job would turn from God. Note that God is always in control and merely allowed this testing to take place because He knew his servants heart. In fact in the end God replaced everything that Job had lost. And although Job complained he never cursed God.

Satan that makes God children to commit sin and disobey God is known by many names throughout the bible, examples-

- The tempter – Mathew 4:3, 1 Thessalonians 3:5
- Ruler of demons – Mathew 9, 34, marks 3:22, Luke 11:15
- Evil one – Mathew 13:38, 1 John 5:19
- The father of Lies – John 8:44
- Ruler of this world – John 12:31
- The ruler of the darkness of this age – Ephesians 6:12
- An adversary – 1 peter 5:8
- The accuser – Revelations 12:10
- The serpent and dragon – Revelations 12:9, 3:17, 13:2, 11
- A roaring lion seeking who to devour – 1 peter 5:8

Although Satan may like to believe that he has control of this world and that in turn he has somehow attained the godhood that he sought, we must remember that he is not co-equal with God, even though he does not realize it; he remains a subject of the sovereign will of God. It is important to know that Satan has already lost. We know that through the crucifixion, death and resurrection of Christ - the Son of God - Our Lord and Savior, Satan is a defeated enemy. His days are numbered, his fate is sealed. Does this raise the question of whether or not God is responsible for creating evil? The answer is no! because right from the onset the angelic hosts had free will and so the evil that was given birth to was not by creation, or by the design of God, but by the desire of one created being and the festering of his evil thoughts and rebellious actions against the father, Lucifer is indeed the first instance of direct rebellion against

God that begins to paint a picture of what sin is and what it will become.

Therefore, as sin first entered Gods creation through the prideful thoughts of one of His created beings, so now, through Satan's Influence sin entered Gods newest creation Mankind. Adam and Eve would eventually rebel against God through their direct disobedience of God instructions and requirements, in other words, against Gods clearly stated will and purpose. Adam and Eve in their innocence were deceived by the enemy of God and fell for it. Day after day, Satan continues to work against us, tempting us and roaring like a lion seeking who he will pounce on and devour next. Sadly, although we see it happening around us, we do nothing about it and simply go about our lives continuing in our own active rebellion against God. We see brothers and sisters in Christ fall and even those who do not yet know him get devoured and we do nothing to save them. We forget that the consequence of disobedience is always the judgment of God against our rebellion and insubordination.

The Old Testament for most part is the account of how God moved and worked in and through His people. But it also records the continual willful disobedience of His chosen people, Israel. Time after time and prophet after prophet, the sermon was always the same repent and return to God. The people of God rebelled against God time and time again they failed to trust God and so they spent 430 years in captivity plus another 40 years wondering in the desert. The Journey could have been made in less than two weeks, believe it or not, but as the consequence of their sin, they were conquered and scattered and persecuted and killed, and all of it can be accredited to their mistrust and insubordination to God's plan for them. The scriptures tell us that

> *"God knew us, in fact knitted us together in our*
> *mother's womb." (psalm 139:13)*

"God has a plan and a purpose for each of us, a plan that will not harm us but rather bring us hope and a future." (Jeremiah 29:11)

The Effect of Sin in a Christian's Life

While it is true that a Christian is a forgiven sinner, and the blood of Jesus Christ has paid for his sins, there are still consequences in the present life. Every time we sin, we do miss the mark. God has set high standards for us all because he is just and deserving of our obedience. It is because we have missed the mark that Jesus died. His blood covers every single sin. What happens, though, when we do sin? What are the consequences of Sin? Let us review the bible and see what it has to say.

Separation

"But your iniquities have made a separation between you and your God." (Isaiah 59: 2a)

This is by far the biggest consequences of sin. Every sin is an offense to God, and God cannot be in the presence of sin. That is why if you choose to keep committing the same sins without repentance, you will stop feeling His presence in your life. The Holy Spirit will stop speaking to you if you refuse to repent.

"Do not quench the spirit? (1 Thessalonians 5:19)

How do you quench the spirit?

"Do not despise prophecies, but test everything, hold fast to what is good. Abstain from every form of evil." (1 Thessalonians 5:20-22)

If you take to heart and apply these verses to your life, you will hear God speaking through the Holy Spirit in your life

Sin is Harmful to You

The following stories are extreme, but it shows you how far your sin can take you. Sodom and Gomorrah were two of the most reprehensible cities known to man. They filled with sin that God could no longer hold back his wrath. God knew that Lot and his wife were dedicated to Him, so he sent 2 angels to warn them to leave before the destruction of the cities.

> *"And as they brought them out, one said, Escape for your life. Do not look back or stop anywhere in the valley. Escape to the hills, lest you be swept away" (Genesis 19:17)*

Lot understood and obeyed. He took his wife and daughters out of the city. He tried to get his future son-in-laws to flee too, but they thought he was joking. When they were out of the city, Lot's wife could not resist the temptation to sin and look back. What happened?

> *"But Lot's wife behind him, looked back and she became a pillar of salt." (Genesis 19:26)*

Lot's wife lost her life because of that one sin. God takes sin seriously, which is why we should always choose His way, instead of our own way.

Sin is Harmful to Others

When one chooses to run his or her life independent of God, catastrophic events can happen. King Herod was an evil man, full of selfish ambitions. He was troubled when he heard Jesus was born. (Mathew 2:3), He discovered where Jesus was born, but God being Omniscient (all knowing) led Jesus away safely through Joseph and Mary to Egypt. Herod's rage led to massive destruction after he realized that Jesus had been led out of Bethlehem.

> *"Then Herod, when he realized that he had been tricked by the wise men, became furious, and he sent and killed all the male children in Bethlehem and in that entire region who were two years old or under." (Mathew 2:16)*

Herod's sin cost the life of many innocent children

Sin is a Catalyst for More Sin

As believers, it is the Holy Spirit that convicts us when we do wrong (John 16:7-8); so that we can repent and be clean again. However, in the case of unbelievers or believers who refuse to repent, sin can catapult us into deeper sin. How does adultery happen? It doesn't just happen; it is a sin by sin process. It starts with a look, "wow that person is very attractive" (you should be focused on your spouse) if you feed that thought then it escalates, "Talking to them isn't going to hurt anything." (You should be thinking about your spouse) that won't be enough. Now you are attracted physically and some-what emotionally, "I can't stop thinking about him/her." (You should be thinking about your spouse). Then you are in deep water, your sexual drive will overtake you without confessing your sin. Satan knows how to reel anyone in. he has mastered it. If we don't take sin seriously, we will end up committing a multitude of sins that started from only one thought.

Sin is an Eternal Death Sentence to Unbelievers:

"For the wages of sin is death" (Romans 6:23).

A true believer will repent of their sins, but those who are rebellious are in serious trouble! Eternal death (separation from God forever) awaits all who choose to not accept Christ as their Lord and Savior. Christ himself says in Mathew 25:41-46 what will happen to those who do not show Christ's love to humanity. Those who do not feed the hungry, cloth the naked visit the sick and people in prison, or give a drink to the thirsty will be left alone in utter torment for eternity. The self-seeking, proud, pompous, self-righteous and greedy people will not be in heaven unless they repent. If you are an unbeliever reading this book, know that God loves you and this is how I know:

> *"The Lord is not slow to fulfill his promise, as some count slowness but is patient toward you, not wishing that any should perish, but that all should reach repentance." (2 Peter 3:9)*

I urge you, if you have not accepted Christ as your Lord and savior, to wait no longer. Tomorrow is not guaranteed. Note that sin has more consequences than the ones that I have analyzed, sin is always destructive, but repentance is always constructive.

How Can a Christian Strive to Live a Sin-Free Life?

Is it possible for a Christian to live without sinning? Nowhere in the bible does it say that a Christian in this life will ever be completely perfect, that is free from all sin. As long as we are on earth, we will always struggle against temptation and sin. That is one reason Jesus taught His disciples to pray (in the Lord's Prayer),

> *"Forgive us our sins... And lead us not into temptation, but deliver us from the evil one"* (Luke 11:4, Mathew 6:13).

Sometimes we sin by our actions, sometimes by our motives; often we sin because of what we do, or fail to do. For example, we fail to love or forgive others, or in other ways fail to do things we ought to do, and that is sin, because we sin does not mean we are no longer Gods Children. Our fellowship with God may be broken, but our relationship is not, and note when we sin God stands ready to forgive us, and we need to turn to Him immediately.

> *If we confess our sins, God is faithful and just*
> *and will forgive us our sins and purify us from*
> *all unrighteousness." (1 John 1:9)*

God also wants to help us to avoid sin In the future

> *"live by the spirit and you will not gratify the*
> *desires of the sinful nature."*

We should always thank God that we belong to Christ and thank him for His grace and forgiveness whenever we do sin and for the strength to overcome future temptation.

The most important point in this paragraph is the Christian faith, which teaches us in general that sin cannot be overcome through human ingenuity or effort. The solution to the problem lies in what God has done for us through Jesus Christ. The penalty for sin is death, judgment, and hell, but the gospel is that God has chosen to pay this penalty himself in the sacrificial life and death of his son Jesus. (John 3:16, Acts 20:28, Romans 3:21-26, 5:6-10, Corinthians 5:18-19, Colossians 2:13-15) through Christ atoning sacrifice on cavalry He set humankind free by taking the retribution of sin upon himself. He suffered the agony and shame that we deserve to suffer because of our sin. He thereby satisfied the just requirement of Gods law and at the same time turned away God's wrath from fallen humankind. His sacrifice was both an expiration of our guilt and Gods sight in that Christ righteousness is imputed to those who have faith likewise, it represents the sanctification of sinners by virtue of their being engrafted into Christ's body through faith. The Cross and resurrection of Christ also accomplish the redemption of sinners, because they have been brought back out of slavery of sin into the new life of freedom.

SALVATION

What is Salvation? Salvation is being saved or protected from harm, or being saved or delivered from some dire situation. This word carries the idea of victory, health, or preservation. Biblical salvation is Gods way of providing his people deliverance from sin as earlier discussed and spiritual death through repentance and faith in Jesus Christ. In the Old Testament the concept of salvation is rooted in Israel's deliverance from Egypt in the book of Exodus. The New Testament reveals the source of salvation is in Jesus Christ. By faith in Jesus Christ, believers are saved from God's Judgment of sin and its consequences, which is eternal death

Why Salvation?

When Adam and Eve rebelled, man was separated from God through sin. God's holiness required punishment and payment (atonement) for sin, which was eternal death. Our death is not sufficient to cover the payment for sin. Only a spotless sacrifice, offered in just the right way can pay for our sin. Jesus, the perfect God-man, came to offer the pure. Complete and everlasting sacrifice to remove, atone, and make eternal payment for sin. Why? Because God loves us and desires an intimate relationship with us. There are different reasons one should strive for salvation is as follows

Assurance of Salvation

If one felt a "tug" of God on the heart, one can have the assurance of salvation. By becoming a Christian, you will take one of the most important steps in your life on earth and begin an adventure unlike any other. The call of salvation begins with God. He initiates it by wooing or drawing us to come to him. After we are drawn to God, we confess an acceptance of God's gift of salvation by praying a salvation prayer.

Salvation Prayer

You want to make your response to Gods call of salvation in prayer, is simply talking with God. You can pray by yourself, using your own words. There is no special formula. Just pray from your heart to God and He will save you. After you have finished saying the salvation prayer, get to know the Savior better. Jesus Christ is the central figure in Christianity and His life, message and ministry,

> *"Everyone who calls on the name of Jesus Christ is secured and saved." (Romans 10:13)*

> *"He saved us, not because of works done by us in righteousness, but according to his own mercy, by washing of regeneration and renewal of the Holy Spirit, whom he poured out on us richly through Jesus Christ our savior, so that being justified by his grace we might become heirs according to the hope of eternal life." (Titus 3:3-7)*

It is important to note that after one has accepted Jesus Christ as the Lord and Savior, there is still a journey ahead, from the acceptance of Christ and death. And this is the only path that leads to eternal life (Romans 6:20-23), and is walked by faith alone, in the power of the Holy Spirit (Romans 8, Galatians 3:2-5). It contains bumps, struggles and setbacks, but is marked by growth in love for others and God. It involves the fight of faith, a striving for peace and holiness (Hebrew 12:14,

1 John 1:9) and reoccurring approach of the throne of grace (Hebrews 4:16).

"Our lord Jesus Christ will sustain you to the end, guiltless in the day of our lord Jesus Christ. God is faithful, by whom you were called into the fellowship of his Son, Jesus Christ our Lord." (1 Corinthians 1:7-9)

I submit to you that I am going to heaven, not because I go to Soul Reapers Worship Center International, not because I attend Church every Sunday, not because I have been baptized, or pay my tithes, not because I try to live right. All of these things are good and every saved person ought to do them, but those things cannot save the soul. I am going to heaven because one day I came to a point in my life where I looked to no one or nothing else but to Jesus Christ alone. I am going because I know Jesus Christ and I have walked with him. One thing and one thing alone was required for me to be saved and I did that thing. I looked to Jesus Christ and he saved my soul. And he is the author and finisher of my faith.

"My soul is built on nothing less

Than Jesus blood and righteousness.

I dare not trust the sweetest frame,

But wholly lean on Jesus name. On

Christ the solid rock I stand, all other ground

Is sinking sand, all other ground is sinking sand".

Salvation is the most important thing that a born again Christian will ever have.

> *"That whosoever believeth in him should not perish, but have eternal life (Salvation). For God so loved the world, that he gave his only begotten son, that whosoever believed in him should not perish, but have everlasting life (Salvation). For God sent his Son into the world to condemn the world, but that the world through him might be saved (Salvation). He that believed on him is not condemned, but he that believeth not is condemned already, because he hath not believed in the name of the only begotten Son of God." (John 3:15-18)*

Conclusion

Man, Sin and Salvation has been a big and tremendous journey through the bible for this chapter. In a nut shell, I will give a brief summary of this topic before I go into the final conclusion; God the maker of heaven and earth created man in his image and breathed life into him.

> *"So God created man in his own image, in the image of God created he him, male and female created he them. (Genesis 1:27)*

And man disobeyed God, by this particular disobedience, man sinned against God. And for man to get back to God, he must repent of his sin, and accept Jesus as his Lord and Personal savior, and by so doing will be saved, and have everlasting life (Salvation).

"That whosoever believeth in him should not perish, but have eternal life. For God so loved the world that He gave his only begotten Son, that whosoever believeth in him should not perish, but have everlasting life. For God sent not his son into the world to condemn the world, but that the world through him will be saved. (John 3:15-17)

Finally the coming of our Redeemer

"But when the fullness of time , God sent forth his Son, made of a woman, made under the law, to redeem them that were under the law, that we might receive the adoption of sons." (Galatians 4:4-5)

The sacrifice of Jesus Christ was needed to save mankind. By the shedding of his blood on the cross of Calvary, we were deeded an unmerited gift of salvation; which means that the work of salvation was outside of man's own hand, and all born of Adam inherited Adams' fallen nature, which was prone to sin. God could have chosen to let man perish or to destroy the devil totally there and then. Instead, God single handedly crafted a plan to save man from his fallen nature and from the power and penalty of sin. God sent a Redeemer, Jesus Christ, the perfect Sacrifice (Man + Sin = Sinful man. Jesus Christ + Sinful man = SALVATION)

Dealing with Death in a Death-filled World

Introduction

This particular topic is a very important subject matter but people living always try to circumvent this subject, while many go as far as brushing the subject matter aside. Nevertheless, I chose to dedicate this chapter to the discussion of death and all that is associated with it. Death is a fact of life that cannot be escaped, because it is a sure appointment that all human kind must keep,

> "And it is appointed unto men once to die, but after this judgment" (Hebrews 9:27).

Death is defined as the cessation of all biological functions that sustain a living organism. The phenomena that commonly bring about death includes, biological aging, predation, malnutrition, disease, suicide, homicide, starvation, dehydration and accidents or trauma resulting in terminal injury. The etymology of Death: the word death comes from old English dead, which in turn comes from Proto-Germanic Dauthuz (reconstructed by etymological analysis). This comes from the Proto-Indo-European stem dheu – meaning the "process, act, condition of dying."

Death to all living things is something that cannot be fought off,

> *"For that which befalleth the sons of men befall-*
> *eth beasts, even one thing befalleth them: as the*
> *one dieth, so dieth the other, yea, they have all*
> *one breath, so that man hath no preeminence*
> *above a beast: for all is vanity, (Ecclesiastics*
> *3:19)*

This substantiates the fact that death is inevitable, we cannot hide or shy away from it. But for a Christian believer, who has accepted Christ as his or her Lord and personal savior, death is the beginning of eternal Life as promised unto us by God,

> *"For God so loved the world that he gave his*
> *only begotten Son, that whosoever believeth in*
> *Him should not perish, but have everlasting*
> *life." (John 3:16)*

That particular verse is the hope of a born again Christian. From a scriptural perspective, death is not a prominent thing, there are so many people in the bible who died without ever being mentioned. Such people include: Mathew, Peter and John etc, death is seen as a positive thing in the scriptures because it is through death that a righteous man can gain everlasting life. Death is a permanent thing and no one knows the day he or she will die. It is an unavoidable and ephemeral process affecting all mankind. However, death is viewed differently by those who have faith in God.

> *"And I heard a voice from heaven saying unto me, write, blessed are the dead which die in the Lord from henceforth: yea, saith the Spirit, that they may rest from their labors, and their works follow them. (Revelations 14:13)*

For a righteous man's death is seen as a fearless thing, a precious thing, a hopeful thing, a triumphant thing, a divine element, and great gain in the body of Christ.

The Origin of Death From the Scriptural View

In the beginning of time, when God created man (Adam and Eve) in his own image and he put them in the garden of Eden, man sinned by disobeying God (by eating the forbidden fruit) God cursed man, and death entered into the world. This means that all human beings must die, and there are two forms of death;

(1) Physical death: this is the separation of the soul from the body, which is as a result of sin (disobedient of Adam and Eve). Therefore death is an acquired trait and is not the natural destiny of man, the body must die and will return back to the dust from which it is made from. When this body dies, the soul comes out, because it was the breath of God that He used to create man, meaning that the soul lives on, though the physical body is dead.

> *"And the Lord formed man off the dust of the ground, and breathed into his nostrils the breath of life; and man became a living soul"* *(Genesis 2:7).*

All souls are Gods', and the soul that sin must die, from the scriptures it is talking about the second death which is applicable that all that rejected Jesus as their Lord and Personal savior.

> *"Behold all souls are mine; as the soul of the father, so also the soul of the son is mine: the soul that sinneth, it shall die" (Ezekiel 18:4).*

(2) The second kind of death is the death of the soul. The only way out of the soul death or second death is by salvation through Jesus Christ, there is no other way out of this.

> *"For God so loved the world, that he gave his only begotten son, that whosoever believeth in him should not perish, but have everlasting life" (John 3:16).*

This everlasting life is all the born-again Christians are looking forward to, so that they can avoid the death of the soul (being sent into hell). You just have to trust that Jesus died for your sins in other to avoid this.

The Death of the Righteous

For a righteous man, death is an awesome thing because he has hope for eternal life; he has been with the Lord fervently while living, the righteous man will still be with the lord after death. "For whether we live, we live unto the Lord, and whether we die, we die unto the Lord: whether we live therefore or die, we are the Lords. After the death of a righteous man, he has a lot to gain in eternal glory, some of the things gained will be as listed below:

1. Celestial Palace: after the righteous man's death, he will gain a celestial palace, a mansion not made with

hands, 2 Cor 5:5, when a righteous man dies he will gain, a great mansion in heaven, a house built high above all the visible orbs, bespangled with light, and filled with pearls and precious stones. Col 1:12, Rev 21:19

2. Glorious Sight of God: after the righteous man's death, he will see the glorious sight of God and he will enjoy God's love in a face-to-face encounter. There shall be no more veil on God's face, he shall experience the love that passes knowledge, and this will cause a jubilation, that surpasses any jubilation in their life time.

3. Fearless Destination: the death of a righteous man is a fearless thing. "Yea, though I walk through the valley of the shadow of death, I will fear no evil, thou art with me, they rod and thy staff they comfort me" (Psalms 23:4)

4. Triumphant Victory: the death of a righteous man is a triumphant thing; "And it came to pass that the beggar died and was carried by the angels into Abrahams bossom and the rich man also died and was buried, and in hell he lift up his eyes being in torments and seeth Abraham afar off, and Lazarus in his Bossom" (Luke 16:22-23)

5. Royal Magnificent Feast: the death of the righteous will gain a royal magnificent feast. They shall hunger no more because they will be feeding from the tree of life (Rev. 22:2)

6. Perfection in Holiness: the death of the righteous man brings perfection of holiness.

The righteous man will gain all this at death because through the work of salvation, he has earned the right to all the heavenly privileges, as an heir to the inheritance of God the father.

"And if children, then heirs; heirs of God, and joint-heirs with Christ; if so be that we suffer with him, and that we may also be glorified together." (Romans 8:17)

And also we should know that at death, God rescued the righteous man from the Kingdom of darkness, wickedness, envy, etc and he has brought us into the Kingdom of His dear son, Jesus Christ, (Colossians 1:12-13). From here, we have seen all the righteous man will gain at death, this chapter will not be complete without looking at what the unbeliever or wicked man will gain after death.

The Death of the Wicked

As we have seen above, the righteous are great gainers and on the opposite, the wicked are the great losers. There is no middle ground as we analyze the four main things the wicked will definitely lose.

1. Loss of the Soul: the wicked will lose their souls, "For what is a man profited, if he shall gain the whole world, and lose his own soul? Or what shall a man give in exchange for his soul" (Mathew 16:26) the souls of the wicked are taken to hell and will be tormented.

2. Loss of the World: the wicked will lose the world that is a great loss for the wicked, because they have laid up their treasure in earth, and to be turned out of it in death.

3. Loss of Heaven: the wicked will lose heaven. Heaven is a place of royal seat of the blessed; it is the region of happiness, the map of perfection. In heaven there is a garden of spices, the bed of perfumes, the rivers of pleasure, the streets of Gold etc, the wicked at death will surely lose all these.

4. Loss of Eternal Hope: at death, the wicked will lose all hope. Though the wicked lived wickedly, they hoped God would be merciful, and they hoped they would go to heaven, their hope is in vain. At death, they lose their hopes, knowing they had ample opportunities to repent, but played themselves into hell. Such destiny await all those that forget God, so perishes the hope of the godless, what he trusts in is fragile, all his hopes are in vain, Job 8:13-14. "The hope of the Godly results in happiness, but the expectation of the wicked is all in vain", (Proverbs 10:28). "When a wicked man dieth, his expectation shall perish: and the hope of the unjust men perisheth"(proverbs 11:7), "the desire of the righteous will always end in good, but the hope of the wicked only in wrath". (Proverbs 11:23).

We have seen all the meaning, facts about death, what the righteous man will gain and what the wicked man will lose after death, how then can we avoid the subject matter of death, which is something everyone must experience.

Always Prepare for Death

It is true that when one knows in his heart that death is near, he starts to live. For the child of God, the preparation of death is in the living of life.

> *"In those days Hezekiah sick unto death, and the prophet Isaiah the son of Amoz came to him, and said unto him, Thus saith the Lord, set thine house in order, for thou shalt die and not live" (2 Kings 20:1).*

We should always set our house in order at all times, it can mean the following (finances, children, projects, will and testament etc) and we should also set our soul in right standing with God at all times.

> *"And it is appointed unto men once to die, but after this judgment" (Hebrews 9:27).*

We should always live faithfully to the true God; being faithful to Him at all times will definitely guarantee us a place in heaven, in his eternal gory. And we should always live in the fear and awe of God, because God is not partial.

> *"And if ye call on the father, who without respect of persons judgeth according to every man's work, pass the time of your sojourning here in fear" (1 Peter 1:17).*

So in everything we do on earth, we should do it with the fear of the Lord, and we should know in our mind that no one can live wrong and die right, there is no opportunity for repentance or salvation after death.

How We Should View Death

Most people are afraid to die, but the most certain truth is that we all will die someday. As a born again believer in Christ, we should deal with death or dying as people that have hope for the eternal glory. Death should be viewed as a positive phenomena and the only bridge that crosses from planet earth into eternity with Christ. Death is a departure, and occurs when the spirit leaves the body. At the cross-road of death, the body is "losed down "and the spirit man is "losed up" for example when Lazarus died, his spirit was carried away by the angels into Abrahams bosom" (Luke 16:22). Death in Christ is a reunion with the righteous loved ones, and a reunion with the Lord. And on the other hand for the wicked, death is the beginning of an eternity of suffering, and if you are not sure that you will be with Christ when you die or you have not accepted God as your Lord and personal savior, Just trust that Jesus died for your sins, and confess with your mouth that Jesus is Lord and believe in your heart that God raised Him from the dead, you will be saved (Romans 10:9), and you can go ahead and say this simple and short salvation prayer.

> *Dear God, I know that I am a sinner. I believe that Jesus died to forgive me of my sins. I now accept your offer of eternal life. Thank you for forgiving me all my sin. Thank you for the new life, from this day forward, I will choose to follow you, forever and ever. Amen.*

Once you have said this prayer, whole heartedly in faith, believe it. You are now a born again Christian, (Eph 2:8) and should not be afraid of losing your soul, because we are now one with Christ and even after life on earth, we will reign with Him in his eternal glory.

Dealing with Depression in a Depressing World

Daily, people are consumed with bad news, facing problems in their homes, financial difficulties, sickness and many other struggles of life, so it is not surprising that there are so many people battling depression in this world. Depression is one of the leading causes of physical death today, as we mentioned above.

What is depression? The word depression is used to cover a whole range of feelings from a fleeting sense of unhappiness to profound, enduring, suicidal hopelessness. We all have ups and downs each day that are usually related to the frustrations and disappointment of normal life. A sense of dejection colors our thought and activities for hours or even days as we come to terms with a broken relationship, a failed exam, lack of promotion at work, the loss of a job, or plans foiled by other unexpected circumstances. Some people cycle in and out of moods of happiness and sadness with dramatic speed and intensity for all to see, others more placid by temperament, experience little outward variation in mood. There are people who reside at the ends of the spectrum, those who are consistently exuberant and enthusiastic , rarely appearing unhappy, while others are consistently depressive and melancholic, rarely seeming happy, but most of the time, most of us will live with a range of experiences of happiness and sadness and we will rarely hit the dark places of despair and hopelessness of the wild excesses and disinhibition of mania, and depression occurs in every culture, but it might be often described differently.

Are Christians Immune from Depression?

Christians are not exempted from these symptoms of depression or neither depressing times nor have God's people ever been exempt from discouragement and depressing times. If we think that as children of God, we are immune from the hardship and challenges of life, then we deceive ourselves. Note that people like Moses, Elijah, David and Jonah experienced some form of depression in their life time, and we can see this from the kind of prayers these men prayed to God, and I believe most of these prayers were made to God because of physical exhaustion, as they were worn out. For example in Numbers 11:11,

> *"Moses said unto the Lord Wherefore hast thou afflicted thy servant? And wherefore have I not found favor in thy sight, that thou layest the burden of all this people upon me?"*

This shows that Moses was worn out and weary, he had a lot of responsibilities on him, this really made him stressed out, and from too much stress can come depression, which Moses dealt with. But God being God still brought him out of this misery by making provision for him and all the Israelites at the time of their needs, through Moses' rod he did wonders, and also God gave Moses a staff of men (Numbers 11:16).

Prophet Elijah is another example, despite his incredible faith, he fell into depression going from mountain top to the valley, the last thing one will ever think of, is a great man of God praying to die or being depressed:

> *"But he himself went a day's journey into the wilderness, and came and sat down under a juniper tree: and he requested for himself that he might die; and said, it is enough; now O Lord, take away my life, for I am not better than my fathers" 1 Kings 19:4.*

This verse shows that Elijah was depressed, but him focusing on God and getting a new direction, from God, still made him a unique and incredible Prophet of God, and he still made it to heaven. And the four major things that made him escape this particular depression are as follows:

1. He got some rest (1 Kings 19:5-6).
2. He got a new focus.
3. Had a new expectations (1 Kings 19:11-12).
4. He took obedient actions (1 Kings 19:15).

It is obvious that pressure leads to depression, but how we handle the pressures determines whether we end up in depression or victory. Note that the ultimate prescription for Elijah was rest, refocus, accurate expectations, and obedient actions, and all these remedies are applicable to believers in the present day. Hence, apply the four steps as applied by Elijah, will help us combat the spirit of depression.

In Psalms 6:6-7,

"I am weary with my groaning, all the night make I my bed to swim, I water my couch with tears, mine eye is consumed because of grief; it waxeth old because of all mine enemies."

As we can see from this verses, grief can cause depression, as in David's situation. But king David took certain steps from depression to victory, and the steps include:

1. **Praying to God at all times.**

2. **He had a heart of gratitude; he was always grateful to God, (Phil. 4:7).**

Gratitude to God goes a very long way towards eliminating depression, if we turn our minds to God's mercy, goodness, and grace we are much better able to deal with stress and depression.

3. **David was always singing, and rejoicing in the Lord, and this made him to be named "a man after Gods own heart" (Acts 13:22), and he earned this title because King David always repented of his sin with great remorse, he always begged God to forgive him and restore him to His favor (Psalms 139:23-24).**

If we follow King David's footsteps, we will be far away from depression, because we will have a clean heart before the Lord at all times. Though David wrote Psalms about great sorrows, his heart was always focused on God. He always asked God for forgiveness, and maintained a heart free from any guilt; which led God to call him his friend. If we aligned our heart with God at all times, we will definitely be called a friend of God as David, enjoying a depression-free life. Another case study from the bible was Jonah. Jonah exhibited signs of depression Jonah 4:3:

> *"Therefore now O Lord, take, I beseech thee, my life from me; for it is better for me to die than to live."*

and Jonah 4:8,

> *"And it came to pass, when the sun did arise, that God prepared a vehement east wind; and the sun beat upon the head of Jonah, that he fainted, and wished in himself to die, and said it is better for me to die than to live."*

From this two bible verses we can clearly see the signs of depression, Jonah made this statement because God did not carry out His judgment on Nineveh. Nineveh's redemption depressed Jonah, and this was so because Jonah refused to recognize Gods sovereignty, as his mind held unto his human idea of justice. Jonah's behavior was as a result of his anger, being deceived by his emotions, making his depression to deepen. People who are depressed mostly focus on the present situation and circumstances, but it is very important to have in our mind how God worked in the past to find hope for the future.

Just as Jonah did not understand why God was allowing him to suffer, many of us today still look at it that way today, but we should always have in mind, that God knows it all. Why be depressed when God will always take care of us? Ecclesiastes 11: 5:

> *"As thou knowest not what the way of the spirit is, nor how the bones do grow in the womb of*

*her that is with child: even so thou knowest not
the works of God who maketh all".*

Anger blinds clarity, and Jonah was not happy over the
grace God had given to the Ninevites. Hence we can rightly
say that anger fueled his depression. When we are heading
towards depression, we should know that God is a sovereign
God, and we can put all our trust in this sovereign God with full
assurance that He will definitely see us through every storm of
life and resolve our every adversity.

How Can a Christian Avoid to be Depressed

Living through life as believers, we are tempted daily to
backslide to our old ways. The odds are stacked high to cause
us to slip back into the world; that's why we have to daily renew
our minds. We need to be "transformed by the renewing of
your mind" (Romans 12:2) with the broad perspective of what
God is doing in the world and in us. The beginning of this
renewal is a new identity based on the significance, security
and acceptance and hope that we receive in our relationship
with God and with other Christians in the family of God. As we
begin to see things from this point of view, we realize more
and more that our self-esteem cannot depend entirely on what
other people think of us. It must be rooted in Gods view of us.
When we feel like saying I am useless or a failure, we remind
ourselves that this is a lie; reality is that we are loved and accepted with all our failings. As we expose ourselves to the truth
of God's word, our thoughts and attitudes are continuously
challenged and renewed. We begin to have new understanding of our value, purpose and place in the universe, also even
modern neuroscience affirms the biblical reality that this renewal and reintegration process begins as we open ourselves
to relationships with people with whom we can share our life
stories, becoming able to experience and understand our in-
ner emotional life and our habitual response to ourselves, to
people around us and to God. We begin to have new attitudes
towards ourselves, towards others and towards the details and

difficulties of our lives. Emotions begin to stabilize and we are not blown around so much by circumstances or by other people's attitude towards us. We learn how to handle anger, guilt, shame, fear, anxiety and depression more appropriately and sensitively, so that we do not have to be ruled by our runaway emotions or extreme thought.

Our conscience too is cleansed as we are forgiven our sin, a conscience that have been made insensitive by constant abuse can be renewed by the Holy spirit and by a growing awareness of Gods standards revealed through the scripture. A conscience that is weak either under or over sensitive, can be refined, strengthened or made more accurate. The false shaping of our conscience by parents and others is gradually undone as we come to see things more often from Gods point of view. As we daily, hourly, minute by minute affirm Gods truth about ourselves and our situations, and lessen the dominating and controlling factors in our life, mind and emotions will work together in harmony rather than at odds with each other, moving towards full integration of brain, body, mind and heart. Our confidence is in the fact that when we are with God, dwelling in him, this integration and healing will be complete in our spirit, soul and body

Conclusion

Death is a necessary thing and will happen to everyone in his or her life time. There is no escape from it, but the only hope we have is in our Lord Jesus Christ. Death will come and we will live an eternal life through our Lord Jesus Christ and this is the victory over death, because Christ assured us that in His word that this separation (death) is not permanent for believers in Jesus Christ, because one day there must be a reunion of the believing loved ones in heaven and we will never be separated again. In that day, we will enjoy not only fellowship with the Lord, but with other members of Christian family that went to be with the Lord, before us; that will be the victory over death. And this makes it very important for a believer to be steadfast in his faith and believe at all times that Jesus came and died for our sins so that we can eventually overcome death when it comes and make it to heaven.

> *"O death, where is thy sting? O grave, where is thy victory? The sting of death is sin; and the strength of sin is the law, but thanks be to God, which giveth us the victory through our Lord Jesus Christ, therefore, my beloved brethren, be ye steadfast, unmovable, always abounding in the work of the Lord, for as much as ye know that your labor is not in vain but in the Lord"* (1 Corinthians 15:15-58).

And we should have great confidence in Jesus Christ because He came to earth for us and died for our sins (conquered death) and rose again and is with God, that we as believers will conquer death and unite with our Lord and Savior after death on earth.

Hope is a major need for those who are depressed. Hope empowers people to not give up, while the world we are living in offers hope in diverse forms, true hope for those with depression lies in a correct understanding of the sovereignty of God and in the comfort of His words in the bible. There is both independence and comfort in knowing that God is in control of all things and all things have a purpose.

> *"I will be glad and rejoice in thy mercy: for thou hast considered my trouble; thou hast known my soul in adversities"* Psalms 31:7.

Afflictions for a Christian are not in vain. While the person who is struggling may not understand the purpose of the pain, there is hope in knowing that the purpose exists and that God is at work to perfect His will in our lives. Afflictions is common to all men but the extent of the affliction varies, a lot of men and women have struggled throughout the history with depression and also as seen in the bible, people like Elijah, David, Moses etc, but they all overcame, reading their stories and learning how they coped during this trying periods, will help those who see themselves struggling with depression. And we as children of God should know that whatever our situation or struggles we are facing right now, it is just temporary, they are just a passing phase in our lives, and they should not steal our joy and the glory that await us in Christ Jesus.

Most times our suffering and affliction is the only way we show our total dependence on God. He is totally aware that His children face depression sometimes, this situation at times is for a purpose, when we are going through this affliction and depression, we may not know the reason for it, but we can find solace in knowing that God understands and is in control of the very situation. God does not know only the outcome of that situation, but he also knows what we will pass through to get there. A depressed person often feels alone, like no one has gone through what they are going through, also they should know the bible has a lot of examples of people that have been depressed or gone through a lot. People like Moses, Elijah, Jonah, Joseph, Job, dealt with depression, and they bounced back when they knew that God was sovereign and submitted to Him. When they remembered that God was in control, they became hopeful. While reading the word of God and trusting in His sovereignty may not change the symptoms of the depression, it can offer unimaginable hope.

> *"Be of good courage, and he shall strengthen your heart, all ye that hope in the Lord."*
> *Psalms 31:24*

Once our hope is on the Lord and we understand his sovereignty above all things, we shall overcome any situation we find ourselves.

References

David Horton, "The Portable Seminary" Masters Overview in one volume, Bethany House Publishers 2006.

R.T. Kendall, "Understanding Theology Volume 1" The Means of Developing a Healthy Church in the Twenty First Century, Christian Focused Publishers 1996

Allen R.B, "The Majesty of Man: the Dignity of Being Human" rev.ed. Grand Rapids, Kregel 2000

En.wikipedia.org/wiki/Salvation

Lewis Sperry Chafer "Salvation": God's Marvelous Work of Grace. Logos Bible Software

The Bible, King James Version

https://www.quora.com/What-is-the-significance-of-the-lamb-in-Christianity